C11/2)

C000115332

THE USE OF HYMNS

**A Practical Exploration of the place
of Hymnody within the Liturgy**

Alan Dunstan

To
CHRISTIANA

First published in Great Britain in 1990 by
KEVIN MAYHEW LIMITED
Rattlesden, Bury St Edmunds,
Suffolk IP30 0SZ

© 1990 Alan Dunstan

ISBN 0-86209-124-1

Typeset by Ipswich Typographics, Ipswich, Suffolk
Printed and bound in Great Britain by
The Five Castles Press Ltd, Ipswich, Suffolk

CONTENTS

FOREWORD

One of the things which jars in our worship is when the music, and particularly the hymns, seem totally unrelated to either what the preacher has said or to the theme of the day. It is a sad fact that so many of our churches still have their hymns chosen on the basis of what the people are likely to know, and what is a good tune — or at its worst, what the organist or vicar likes best!

No-one who reads Canon Dunstan's book will ever think quite the same again. Having had vast experience over the years in parishes, in theological colleges, in university, and for the last eleven years, at Gloucester Cathedral, and being a hymnologist of very considerable repute, he has made a study of relating hymns to both congregations and occasions in a unique way.

Canon Dunstan has had the habit, in his capacity as Precentor at Gloucester Cathedral, of enquiring from the preacher what he intended to preach about, some weeks in advance, and then choosing the hymns to suit that particular theme. This has made an enormous difference to the quality and depth of worship, and in this book, which is of tremendous practical usefulness to anyone concerned with the arrangement of worship, there is a fund of experience and knowledge which clergy and lay people will find invaluable.

The Use of Hymns should be compulsory reading for all who are concerned with worship in our churches and the evangelistic and pastoral opportunities which that worship presents.

January 1990   ERIC EVANS
                                                                Dean of St Paul's

INTRODUCTION

This book is offered to those who have the task of choosing hymns for public worship, and to all who are concerned about the use of hymns in liturgy and devotion. It is a successor to *These Are The Hymns* published in 1973 as a guide to the use of hymnody in Anglican worship. Since that date there have been many new liturgies and many new hymn-books; and although several books contain lists of hymns appropriate to the Sunday themes, there is little other help available to those who are regularly involved in their selection.

It is no longer desirable to write about liturgy from a narrowly denominational point of view, and this book is meant to be ecumenical in character. It would be impertinent of me to suggest how hymns should be used throughout the Christian Church; but I write as an Anglican with a close association with Methodism, and fair aquaintance with the Reformed churches in this country. I hope that the principles and suggestions of this book may be useful to Christians of many traditions and many hymn-books, and that it may help them to make the best use of hymnody in their churches.

Many friends have contributed in some way to this book, but I must make particular mention of Canon Cyril Taylor. Not only has he given generously of his time, and encouragement to this project; but he kindly read through the first draft of the manuscript, and I have been able to incorporate many of his valuable suggestions in the text. The dedication is a small expression of all that I owe to my dear wife, whose love and concern have supported me 'through many dangers, toils and snares'.

ABBREVIATIONS

A M N S	Hymns Ancient and Modern — New Standard
E H	English Hymnal
H & P	Hymns and Psalms
M P	Mission Praise
N E H	New English Hymnal
A S B	Alternative Service Book
B C P	Book of Common Prayer
J L G	Joint Liturgical Group

I. WHY HYMNS AT ALL?

The young preacher came from an inner-city area, and was addressing a fairly prosperous congregation with which his parish was linked. The occasion was Harvest Thanksgiving, and he invited his listeners to think of harvest in its widest sense — the harvest of people and goodness and justice; he said that the festival ought to be more than thinking of food and singing harvest hymns.

By harvest hymns, he clearly meant those which have come to be traditionally associated with this occasion. And, indeed, these were the hymns sung at the service. It was a Parish Communion, and the first hymn to be sung after the sermon was at the offertory — *We plough the fields*. At the end of the service came *To thee, O Lord, our hearts we raise* — wider in its connotation, but not calculated to send people out in the power of the Spirit.

What happened that day was typical of a great many Harvest Thanksgivings. Perhaps preachers take some theme like that of the young man mentioned above, or they deal with some great contemporary issue such as world hunger, conservation, or our stewardship of what has been entrusted to us. These subjects may be eloquently presented in the pulpit and faithfully echoed in the prayers, but they do not apparently affect the hymns.

Yet there are hymns that concern themselves with these matters — and such hymns have found their way into standard collections. From older hymnody *Lord, her watch thy Church is keeping* refers to the great harvest of Christian mission, and could have fitted the preacher's theme that day; from contemporary hymnody, Fred Pratt Green's *For the fruits of his creation* begins with creation, goes on to speak of our stewardship within it, and has a third verse about the harvests of the Spirit. There are some good harvest hymns that take up the issues which must concern us at such a festival. This is an area in which there is room for more writing, but at least a start has been made.

Why, then, was the choice on that day restricted to *traditional* harvest hymns? In most congregations, people would feel cheated if they were not given an adequate ration of 'old favourites'. Often such services are attended by very occasional churchgoers familiar with a very small number of hymns, and it is alleged that they would be 'put off' by new words and even more by new tunes. If the contemporary message of harvest is effectively proclaimed in the pulpit and reflected in the intercessions, can people not be allowed to go on singing what they know and love?

But hymns provide the main *vocal* participation of the congregation. They have *listened* to the sermon, and, as often as not, they have *listened* to the prayers. But in the hymns, they are *consciously* participating in the action of the liturgy, and through the hymns they can make their response to the reading and preaching of the Word of God. If the hymns are always predictable, and never reflect those aspects of the Word that have been proclaimed in the sermon, how can the congregation's response be an adequate one? They will easily be lulled into false security and sentimentality, and the message which has been proclaimed will have less opportunity of sinking in.

Of course there is a place for traditional hymnody at Harvest Thanksgiving as at all other occasions. The wonder of God in creation and the goodness of God in providence are of continuing and abiding importance. It is no less important that we should sing of these things in the midst of what the Prayer Book calls 'this transitory life'. Hymnody must not be tied to theological or sociological fashion, and, in history, hymns (as well as liturgy as a whole) have protected us from that. Nor must hymnody be always heavy or didactic, and on the occasion of which we have been thinking, there is room for spontaneity and cheerfulness and joy. But the word of God is particular and specific; and surely there are times when our response should be particular and specific — and the response expressed in the texts of the hymns we sing.

The theme, then of this book is the right *use* of hymns. Its concern is that those who choose hymns and those who sing them should understand more clearly what they are doing, and so come to appreciate the purpose of hymns and hymn-singing.

A. What is a hymn?

It is time to come to some definition of the word *hymn*. In his commentary on Psalm 148, St. Augustine wrote:

> *Know ye what a hymn is? It is a song with praise of God. If thou praisest God and singest not, thou utterest no hymn. If thou singest and praisest not God thou utterest no hymn. A hymn then containeth these three things; song and praise, and that of God. Praise, then of God in song is called a hymn.* [1]

In our own time, a hymn has been defined a little more precisely by Erik Routley:

a strophic song on a Christian subject capable of being sung by a congregation . . . not in any sense made up of trained singers.[2]

Routley acknowledged that the word *hymn* has not always corresponded to his definition. The Greek word, which was in use long before the Christian era, could have meant no more than song in praise of some higher good; and for fifteen hundred years of Christian history, it was not used to describe congregational music at worship — in the sense that we now mean.

Hymn-singing in its present form came in with the Reformation — with the chorales of Germany and the metrical psalms of Switzerland. In our own country, bursts of hymn-writing and hymn-singing attended both the Evangelical revival of the eighteenth century and the Tractarian movement of the nineteenth. During and after the 1960s, there occurred what has been called a 'hymn explosion'. All these upsurges of congregational song have one thing in common; those who wrote and promoted hymns believed them to be a means by which people could learn and appropriate truths about the nature and purpose of God — for themselves and for the world. Surely they have been proved right. The hymn has been shown to be a memorable kind of Christian statement. Hymns stay in the mind when other expressions of the Christian faith have been forgotten.

So for the purpose of this book, we will think of the hymn as a 'strophic song on a Christian subject'. We will think of hymnody as the material collected in what we call hymn-books. Later on we may be disposed to define the word more narrowly: to make a distinction between metrical psalms and hymns; or between hymns and songs; or between hymns and carols — and all this after the fashion of some hymn books and of some parts of the Christian Church. But for the most part we shall use the word hymn to describe the metrical material available in our hymn books.

B. The Purpose of hymns

What, then, is the purpose of hymns in Christian worship? I think it is possible to identify a fourfold purpose.

(1) A means of congregational participation.

In the earliest years of the Christian Church, this would have seemed a rather stilted way of putting it. The first Christian generations apparently had no problems about participation. In the first letter to the Corinthians, we find a sketch of Christian worship, included there because of abuses that had arisen in the course of it. St. Paul sums up:

> *When you meet for worship, each of you contributes a hymn, some instruction, a revelation, an ecstatic utterance, or the interpretation of such an utterance.* [3]

Whether it was really open to all the congregation to make such contributions may be questioned; certainly women were discouraged from doing so. But the New Testament does contain fragments of early Christian hymns, and it seems to have been natural for the communities to express their new faith in song.

It is not within the scope of this book to trace the formalisation and clericalisation of worship that developed over the centuries, but merely to note again that hymn-singing as a congregational activity in the course of Sunday worship is a product of the Reformation era. The books of Common Prayer (1549 and 1552) made no provision for such hymns, though earlier than this, a letter from Thomas Cranmer to Henry VIII had envisaged the use of English hymnody. But when the Prayer Book was re-enacted in 1559, it was accompanied in the same year by the Royal Injunctions, and the 49th of these allows:

> *that in the beginning or at the end of common prayers, either at morning or evening, there may be a hymn or such-like song . . . in the best sort of melody or music that may be conveniently devised, having regard that the sentence of the hymn may be understood and perceived.* [4]

The 'hymn or such-like song' envisaged here seems to have been the metrical psalm, and a year later what came to be known as the *Old Version* by Thomas Sternhold and John Hopkins was printed by John Day with the note

> *newly set forth and allowed according to the order appointed in the Quene's Maiesties Iniunctions*

From this time, according to W. H. Frere 'it was natural to regard the book as the ally and colleague of the Prayer Book'[5]. The metrical psalms of the Old Version (and later of the New Version by Tate and Brady) were normally bound up with the Prayer Book itself.

It was through such psalms that congregations made their main vocal contribution to worship. It is true that the Prayer Book provided many opportunities for congregational response and 'said or sung' was included in many of its rubrics; but so long as illiteracy was widespread, it was the clerk who made the responses, and he who 'lined out' the psalm that was to be sung. So although the official liturgy of the Church of England made no provision for hymns, the metrical psalms and paraphrases paved the way for hymnody as a means of congregational participation.

In the decades that followed 1559, there were those who campaigned for further reformation and simplification of worship. The Puritans, as they came to be called, gained ascendancy during the Commonwealth and Protectorate, and after 1662, became organised as English Dissent. Within such bodies, metrical psalms also became the principal means by which the congregation participated in worship. Most Puritans disliked responsive material, and in the discussions about worship that followed the Restoration (culminating in the Savoy Conference) some suggested that the Litany should be turned into 'one long solemn prayer'. For various reasons — practical as well as theological — singing became established more slowly than in the Protestant churches of the continent. The Baptists were particularly suspicious of it. But certainly by the nineteenth century the worship of what we now call the 'Free Churches' tended to be monologues by the minister, interspersed with the singing of hymns by the congregation.

All this is far removed from the contemporary scene both in Anglican and Free Church worship. But it is important to remember that for Anglicans the reading of lessons by lay people, their leading of intercessions, or lay administration of the elements at Holy Communion is relatively recent. It is no less important to remember that set patterns of worship with prayers involving congregational response were, until recently, rare in the Free Churches. All this underlines the importance of hymn-singing in both traditions, and goes to explain why its legacy is still valued.

We have already used the word 'participation' a number of times. It is important to remember that, liturgically, there are other forms of participation, which include the use of the eye and the ear; cathedral evensong is one example of this. But most people have come to expect to open their mouths as well, and hymn singing has encouraged such expectation.

I have written of two main traditions of worship, but this section cannot end without reference to the very remarkable development of hymn-singing in the Roman Catholic Church since the Second Vatican Council. The possibility of hymns and songs for the congregation has now been built into the Mass itself. This is part of a process by which the laity are no longer seen as spectators of a service in which they might be occupied with their own devotions, but are instead encouraged to follow it in their books, and to enter into it with their voices.

(2) A means of underlining doctrine

From our scanty knowledge of New Testament hymnody, it seems that the new songs of Christians celebrated the beliefs that they held, and which later were to be incorporated into the creeds: that the Messiah had come, that he had been crucified, that he was risen and exalted. The office hymns of the mediaeval Church were largely Scriptural in character — in the first place objective and only secondarily concerned with the impact of Christian doctrine upon Christian life. The Scriptural paraphrases of the Reformation sought to preserve those same doctrines.

But there have been those who saw hymnody as a direct method of teaching doctrine, and from these we may select two famous examples. The first is John Wesley who in his preface to the 1780 *Collection of Hymns for the use of the people called Methodists* wrote of it:

> *It is large enough to contain all the important truths of our most holy religion, whether speculative or practical; yea, to illustrate them all and to prove them both by Scripture and reason; and this is done in a regular order ... So that this book is, in effect, a little body of experimental and practical divinity*[6]

Hymns have been peculiarly valued in the Methodist Church, not only because of the high place that they have held in its liturgy and in the private devotion of its members, but because the hymn-book has been seen as a manual of doctrine. When a Methodist theologian expounds a doctrine, it is not long before he starts quoting a hymn.

The second example is Cecil Frances Alexander. It was for her little god-sons, and their better understanding of the Christian Faith that the Creed was expressed in verse. So 'All things bright and beautiful' expounds the phrase 'Maker of heaven and earth'. The much-sung hymns for Christmas and Passiontide fulfil the same function. So does the most laughed-at of all her compositions:

Within the churchyard, side by side
Are many long, low graves;
And some have stones set over them,
On some the green grass waves. [7]

These are but two examples of hymn-writers seeking to expound Christian doctrine. Whole hymn-books have been drawn up with a particular theological stance. It is not difficult to demonstrate that many people's faith has been shaped by the hymns they have known, and some introductions to hymns in the BBC1 programme *Songs of Praise* are evidence of this. It matters, then, that both words and music should express doctrine that is true. *I vow to thee, my country* is sometimes described as a hymn although it would not meet either of the definitions that have been suggested in this chapter. The first verse is a patriotic song, and the second begins with the couplet

And there's another country I've heard of long ago
Most dear to them that love her, most great to them that know.

What is this 'other country'? Is it heaven, or the kingdom of God? Does it help some people to appreciate either? Of course the Holst tune accounts considerably for the popularity of the song, and it is significant that at least two modern hymn books have provided alternative texts for this music.

But few people would want to impose severe doctrinal tests on hymnody. Tom Baker, the former Dean of Worcester, claimed that the services of the *Alternative Service Book* are 'heavily doctrinal in content' and he added:

For one of the main theological purposes of hymnody is to present doctrine in a more extended, and indeed, more lyrical form than is possible in the liturgy itself. The older liturgies needed supplementing in this way. How much greater the need in the case of the new liturgies with the revisers' predilection for the terse, bald, unadorned doctrinal statements, sometimes a whole lot of them on a string, or recited after the fashion of a list of items. [8]

There are some fine modern examples of this more allusive way of writing. Brian Wren's *There's a spirit in the air* (AMNS 515) leads us subtly from 'spirit' to the Holy Spirit; W. H. Vanstone's

Morning Glory (AMNS 496) from 'Love's endeavour, love's expense' to the love of God; and Erik Routley's translation *There in God's garden* (AMNS 514) makes the tree in Revelation 22:2 a symbol of the saving work of Christ. Nor are twentieth century writers the first to discover this way of presenting doctrine in hymns. An older example may be found in a fine hymn by Thomas Binney *Eternal Light* (H&P 458) where the holiness of God, the sin of man, the way of atonement, the work of the Holy Spirit and the promise of eternal life are all presented in unusual style. It is sad that this hymn is virtually unknown among Anglicans who, when looking for credal material, often turn to Newman's *Firmly I believe and truly* (AMNS 118), where apart from the beautiful third verse, beliefs are, as it were, strung out on a line!

(3) A means of expressing experience.

This third purpose of hymnody is closely akin to the second. Indeed, Christian doctrine cannot be expressed in a 'take it or leave it' manner. It must mean something to the person who speaks of it if it is to be convincingly communicated. Hymns have not usually been written in order to secure assent to a set of propositions by the singers — but rather to stimulate faith, to kindle devotion and to strengthen dedication.

It is therefore not possible to draw as sharp a distinction as has sometimes been attempted between the objective and subjective in hymnody. The best hymns usually contain elements of both. They speak of the loving purposes of God, and the response that they should evoke in the believer. Isaac Watts is remembered by Christians of many denominations and traditions when they sing *When I survey the wondrous cross*. But on the same theme, he wrote another hymn — almost, if not as great — which is only just beginning to be more widely known, and which provides an excellent illustration of this point: *Nature with open volume stands* (AMNS 497) has a first verse which, as this line suggests, speaks of the revelation of God in all things; the next two verses show how that revelation is focussed in the Cross; and the last two express the response of the worshipper. Similarly, Charles Wesley could not write a hymn about doctrine without reference to what it meant for us:

> *'Tis mercy all, immense and free,*
> *For, O my God, it found out me.*

It is significant, too, that contemporary writers still want to offer hymns for Christmas and Easter, although it might be argued that there is already a plentiful supply for both festivals. They do this because they want to say what these events mean for them, and could mean for us.

All this is in the Biblical tradition, for in the pages of the Bible we have no knowledge of God except in relation to this world and to men and women within it. But hymns which express experience have their dangers. We can be asked to express emotions which we do not feel, and to affirm forms of spirituality for which we are not ready. We can be led to think that our own discipleship is invalid unless it is put into a language that is not our own. All this makes for second-hand religion, and for unreality in worship. Both are surely to be avoided, and the fear of them has meant that many 'subjective' hymns, particularly of the Victorian era, have been discarded, most notably those which concentrate on weeping, or longing for death. There may well be individuals for whom such sentiments are apposite, but they do not provide material generally suitable for a whole congregation.

Yet in this sensitive area, there are two considerations to be borne in mind. First, there is surely a place for those hymns of aspiration, which speak of states to which we have not attained, but by the grace of God hope to arrive:

Were the whole realm of nature mine
That were a present far too small;
Love so amazing, so divine,
Demands my soul, my life, my all.

Secondly, hymns, of their very nature cannot be prosaic and literal. They must contain poetry and imagery. The great mediaeval hymns about the new Jerusalem have gone out of fashion, perhaps because people have persistently and mistakenly supposed them to be descriptions of the future life and place rather than aspirations after the state which is perfect. Rightly understood, we can still sing:

O sweet and blessed country
Shall I ever see thy face?
O sweet and blessed country,
Shall I ever win they grace?

Exult, O dust and ashes,
The Lord shall be thy part
His only, his for ever,
Thou shalt be, and thou art!

(4) A means of supplementing liturgy

As we have seen, the Royal Injunctions provided for singing — interpreted as metrical psalms — before and after common prayers, and it later became common to sing them before and after the sermon. During the singing of the first, the priest retired in order to change from his surplice into the Geneva gown, which was the customary vesture for preaching until the later part of the nineteenth century. Nowhere do we find directions about which psalms should be sung, and evidence shows that their selection was often made by the clerk. Not until the nineteenth century were hymns built into the Anglican liturgy itself. Hymns at the Eucharist (as distinct from Ante-Communion) came later still, because the sung Eucharist represents the full flowering of the Catholic revival. In *The Parson's Handbook* Percy Dearmer wrote in some detail about the use of hymns at the Eucharist, and his words reflect an attitude towards them that is still prevalent:

> *A hymn may be sung (1) for a procession (when the Litany is not so used); (2) for the Introit because this is before the commencement of the service; (3) for the Sequence between the Epistle and Gospel — an excellent place from the liturgical point of view — because here there is a necessary interval; (4) at the Offertory, because there is a break in the service; (5) during the Communion, for the same reason; (6) during the Ablutions, because it is at the end of the service, and for the best practical reasons. Thus six hymns may be sung in all, or fewer, according to the needs of the church.*[9]

Few people have done so much for the Anglican hymnody as Dearmer, and elsewhere he had wise and useful things to say about the choice of hymns. But this quotation illustrates an attitude which sees hymns as an embellishment to liturgy. In no way do they supply something that would otherwise be missing. There have, of course, been some exceptions. In the chapel of Pusey House, Oxford, it was the custom for some years to sing *Wherefore, O Father* (EH 335) directly after the 1662 consecration prayer in order to supply what were considered to be the deficiencies of that prayer. In *These Are The Hymns*, I suggested that in the 1662 service, the post-communion hymn might reflect the character of whichever post-communion prayer had been omitted.[10] But hymns have not generally been chosen with that sort of precision.

The rubrics of the *Alternative Service Book* suggest places where hymns might be sung. But they are always optional, and the service in no way depends upon them. The same is true of the Roman Catholic Mass — despite the usual and sometimes enthusiastic inclusion of them. Nevertheless, an American writer has recently claimed of both the English and American services:

> *It is clear that these revised liturgies now recognise music and especially hymns as an integral and necessary part of worship in the Anglican tradition.* [11]

It is noteworthy that the inclusion of hymns in the American liturgy goes back to their 1789 Prayer Book.

In the worship of the English Free Churches, hymns have had a different function. As we have noted, singing was introduced cautiously; but it was Isaac Watts from the Independent tradition, whose work marks the transition from strict paraphrases of Scripture to the freer kind of hymn. By the nineteenth century, the hymn had become an integral and indispensable feature of Dissenting worship. To this tradition the Methodists belong (though they are not Dissenters in the same sense as the old denominations) and to this tradition they have made a most significant contribution.

Thus Bernard Manning, himself a Congregationalist, but a great admirer of Methodist hymnody wrote:

> *We mark times and seasons, celebrate festivals, express experiences and expound doctrines by hymns*

and in the same chapter had said:

> *Hymns are for us Dissenters what liturgy is for the Anglican. They are the framework, the setting, the conventional, the traditional part of divine service as we use it. They are, to adopt the language of the liturgiologist, the Dissenting Use.* [12]

In this tradition, therefore, the hymn does not simply ornament what is there already in worship; it supplies what ought to be there. The hymn is *the* way in which praise is expressed; it is also used as a way of meditating on the Word of God and responding to it; and it may even, in some instances, be the vehicle of the people's penitence or intercession.

These two traditions of hymnody can help and inform each other. How they may do so is the subject of later pages; suffice it to say that the increased use of set liturgies in the Free Churches, and the freer approach to worship among Anglicans suggest new and creative uses of hymns in both.

C. The use and misuse of hymns

(1) The misuse of hymns

The good use of hymns is the theme of this book, but at this stage we can clear the ground with a few points about their misuse. Hymns are misused:

(a) when they are carelessly and insensitively chosen, when there is no regard for such matters as liturgical appropriateness, or relation to the particular theme of the service, and when little care is taken to ensure reasonable variety within the selection.

(b) when they are seen as no more than cover-up operations — when the only consideration for the hymn at the offertory is that it should be long, and the only consideration for a hymn between readings is that it should be short. Three verses before a Gospel reading and two after (to allow the procession to advance and withdraw) is an example of this. A few hymns may lend themselves to this sort of treatment; most do not.

(c) when texts are set to music that is not good enough for them. Some hymns have been made into something quite different from what they were originally by an inspired tune — *For all the saints* to *Sine Nomine* is an outstanding example. Some great texts still await such treatment. The converse is true, but less frequent — when a fine tune is set to indifferent words.

(2) The good use of hymns

Hymns are well used when the selectors really understand what they are for and what they are meant to do at any point in worship for which they are chosen. Erik Routley says that the hymn has done its work when the worshipper can feel 'This is what I wanted to say, but I am grateful to whoever put the words in my mouth'.[13] Most of us can recall occasions when the hymn chosen seemed 'just right'. Such occasions may be rare, but they need not be too rare. For when hymns are 'right' at the time in which they are sung, then they have really come into their own.

NOTES

1. Quoted in Julian, *Dictionary of Hymnology* (John Murray, 1907), p. 640.
2. Erik Routley, *Christian Hymns Observed* (Mowbrays, 1983) pp. 3-4.
3. 1 Corinthians 14:26. Examples of what may be early Christian hymnody are Ephesians 5:14, 1 Timothy 3:16, and some passages used as canticles in the *Alternative Service Book.*
4. Gee and Hardy, *Documents* (1986), p. 435. In 1566, Day was adding to the title page the direction that such psalms might be sung 'before and after sermons', and this has been seen as a raising of their status in the liturgy itself.
5. W.H. Frere, *Historical Edition of Hymns Ancient and Modern,* (1909), p. xliii.
6. The Preface appeared in all editions of Wesley's hymns, and in the *Methodist Hymn Book* (1933). This passage is quoted in the Preface to *Hymns and Psalms,* p. x.
7. *Hymns Ancient and Modern Standard Edition,* no. 575. Some defence of it is offered in Erik Routley, *Hymns and Human Life,* p. 215.
8. Tom Baker, *New Hymns for New Liturgies* (Hymn Society Bulletin, Vol. 9 no. 10), pp. 186-7.
9. Dearmer, *The Parson's Handbook* (Humphrey Milford, 1931), pp. 220-1.
10. Alan Dunstan, *These Are the Hymns* (SPCK, 1973), pp. 32-6 suggests the use of hymns for 'holy Communion — more or less 1662'.
11. Robin A. Leaver and James H. Litton (ed.), *Duty and Delight* (Canterbury Press, 1985), p. 167.
12. B.L. Manning, *The Hymns of Wesley and Watts* (Epworth, 1942), pp. 133-5. The varying use of hymns in different styles of liturgy is discussed further in Cecil Northcott, *Hymns in Christian Worship* (Lutterworth, 1964).
13. Erik Routley, *op. cit.,* p. 107.

II. WHICH HYMN-BOOK?

A. One Hymn Book?

Most congregations think they need only one hymn book, but most congregations find that they cannot remain content with one hymn book.

The campaign for one hymn-book is led by churchwardens, stewards and sidespeople as well as vergers and cleaners. Handing out a library of books to each worshipper is awkward, especially if the congregation is large and if nearly all come at the same time. Conventional church furniture — whether pews or chairs — does not lend itself to much more than two small books. Anything else begins to look messy and untidy. I find that whenever I give a talk on hymnody, someone always asks 'What is the best hymn-book?' or 'Which is the *one* hymn-book you would recommend for this congregation?'

In the 1970s many churches had more than one hymn-book because nearly all standard books had their supplements. For *Hymns Ancient and Modern Revised* there was *One Hundred Hymns for Today;* later, for the *English Hymnal* there was *English Praise;* the Methodists had *Hymns and Songs;* the URC *New Church Praise;* and the Baptists *Praise for Today. Broadcast Praise* appeared in the 1980s as a supplement to the *BBC Hymn Book* as did *Praise and Thanksgiving* for *Hymns for Church and School.* Later standard books have most recently had their own supplements: *Songs of God's People* for the third edition of *The Church Hymnary; Anglican Praise* for the *Anglican Hymn Book;* and *Sing Alleluia* for *With One Voice.*

Alarm bells began to sound when the A & M publishers produced a second supplement in 1979 — *More Hymns for Today,* even though they soon offered the two supplements in one volume. The campaign for 'one hymn-book' was intensified. So the 1980s have seen the production of new standard collections — of which *Hymns Ancient and Modern New Standard,* the *New English Hymnal* and *Hymns and Psalms* are all examples. Work is in progress for a new book for the URC and another for the Baptists. *Hymns for Today's Church* is like Melchizedek, without parentage, and was claimed as the natural accompaniment to the *Alternative Service Book.*

But still it seems that one hymn-book will not suffice. There has been growing demand for another kind of hymn or song — something more relaxed, more simple, apparently more contemporary, and depending less upon organ and choir. In many churches, this was first represented by *Sound of Living Waters* and *Fresh Sounds*. Collections of hymns in this tradition have proliferated in recent years as a glance at the shelves of shops will show. Probably the most widely used is *Mission Praise* which arose out of the Mission England campaign. Here is a mixture of traditional hymnody and 'choruses' so that, for example, *Majesty* is next to *Make me a captive, Lord*. The cheapness of the words edition facilitated its introduction, but it has since had a successor. So the battle about one hymn-book goes on.

Some new standard collections such as *Hymns and Psalms* and *Hymns for Today's Church* include a few songs and choruses, but the representation of this sort of material is hardly enough for those who want it. The demand for new hymnody seems to be always with us, and this is, in fact, an acceleration of a process that has been going on for some time. Older readers will recall the days when *Crimond* was stuck into the back of their hymn-books, or provided on cards by enterprising undertakers.

B. Why so many hymns?

It is worth asking why all this has come about. The 'hymn explosion' is a phrase that has been used to describe the large amount of hymn-writing and the number of hymn-books in the second half of this century.[1] If we vary the metaphor, and think of this output in terms of a river, I would suggest that it has been fed by three streams.

(1) Our changing world

There has been the need to write hymns that in some way reflect the massive changes which have been brought to our society through science, technology and many other disciplines. Thus one of the pioneers of modern hymnody, Albert Bayly, sought to meditate on the mystery of creation in new terms with *O Lord of every shining constellation* or *Lord of the boundless curves of space* (AMNS 411 and 493). A more transient example is *God of concrete, God of steel* (AMNS 366). Alongside this has been the call for hymns which refer to the great issues of our time — such as hunger and housing, world peace and race relations, conservation and ecology. As we saw at the beginning of this book, Harvest Thanksgiving seems to many to be an occasion that cries out for new as well as traditional hymnody.

(2) Liturgical reforms

Hymns have been affected by the widespread liturgical reforms and in particular by the revolution that has occurred in the language of worship. When readings and prayers are all in contemporary English, hymns can remain sole representatives of 'thou' and 'dost'. There are some who find this a total anachronism; but many others who are happy to go on using hymns in their classical form see the need for others in a new style of English, and contemporary writers are certainly using contemporary language for their hymns. But other liturgical changes have added force to this stream of hymn-writing. Most important has been the increased emphasis on eucharistic worship, so that there are few churches of any tradition which do not *sometimes* have a celebration of Holy Communion with hymns and sermon as a 'main' service. And there are liturgical occasions which are new — such as the appointment of the first Sunday after Epiphany for the commemoration of the baptism of Jesus — a renewed link with the Church of the East.

(3) Songs of charismatic influence

There is the style of hymn or chorus that was made popular by the charismatic movement, and various kinds of renewal campaigns, involving the use of instruments other than the organ, particularly guitars — and this has contributed to the considerable library of song-books that we have already noted in this chapter.

C. The needs of a congregation.

So what can be identified as the needs of a congregation for whom a hymn-book (or books!) is to be provided?

(1) 'Conservatives'

There are those for whom liturgy in general and hymnody in particular point to what is enduring in a rapidly-changing world. The hymns they sing are a link between their present and past lives, between themselves as a worshipping community and those who have praised and served God in past centuries. Such people are, by and large, content with standard hymn-books. They may not be totally averse to new texts and new tunes, provided the input of such is rationed and sensitively introduced. This group is familiar in most of our churches, and in many may constitute the majority of the congregation. Ninety per cent of Anglican clergy will say that their parish is 'conservative'.

(2) Children

There are children who have been brought up at school with perhaps a quite different style of singing. Choirmasters have found for a number of years that it is no longer possible to assume that new recruits are familiar with even two dozen standard English hymns. Those who plan worship in churches need a careful and detailed knowledge of what is used and sung in the schools which their children attend.

(3) 'Good standards'

There are those who long for good standards in the texts and music which they sing. I wish I would claim that this group was larger than it is. But there is something very middle-brow about hymnody. People who go to concerts and listen to Radio 3 in their homes happily revert to lower standards in church. Of course they often have no choice. But I was, a few years ago, subjected to some criticism for choosing lesser-known hymns for the opening service of the Three Choirs Festival in Gloucester Cathedral: the music was printed on the service-sheets, and one might have supposed that this was one occasion where a more adventurous approach to hymnody would have been welcomed. Yet a congregation which listened to Howells' anthems was less willing to sing his *Sancta Civitas* to a hymn.

(4) Songs of renewal

There are those who have been led into a lively experience of God through some renewal movement, and have associated that experience with the music of that movement. To such people, what is sung and done in church often seems incredibly stuffy and formal; and although they may be a minority, they are often vocal and determined in their efforts to loosen up worship and to provide an atmosphere that is more relaxed and more capable of attracting newcomers.

Of course people are not so sharply divided as these four categories might suggest. And as we try to think of how to meet the needs of a congregation in which all four are represented, there is one over-riding consideration to be borne in mind. Few people are limited to knowing only those hymns that are sung in the church which they attend. Our society is mobile, and people have attended other churches in the past. The growth of ecumenism means that they may have considerable acquaintance with a denomination or tradition quite different from the one with which they are presently associated. Moreover, the enormous popularity of a programme like *Songs of Praise* means that some hymns and songs never used in their own church will be familiar to some worshippers within it. Because a tune has not been sung there before does not mean that it is 'not known'. It will be hardly necessary to teach *Sing Hosanna* to a congregation that uses only *Ancient and Modern Revised*. Nor will they be quite unfamiliar with *Michael* to *All my hope* if they meet it in another church.

D. Songs and Choruses

It is time to tackle an issue that can be and is divisive in many congregations. This is the whole matter of the hymn in traditional form being set in opposition to the 'song' or 'chorus'. It can mean the resignation of organists and the abandonment of choirs, and it must be acknowledged that there are some who would not be dismayed by the absence of either.

It is important that each 'side' in this issue should try to understand the other's viewpoint. There are those who fear that the 'chorus' will 'take over' as it has tended to do in some Roman Catholic churches where *Celebration Hymnal* is in sole use. It is seen by them as a threat to musical standards and to traditional hymnody. Against this, there are those who feel that conventional worship imprisons the Gospel in a certain culture that appeals only to people who are conditioned by it, and that it is therefore inward-looking and even repressive.

Before going any further, we must remember that the 'song' (which is the word that I will henceforth use for this kind of music that is not cast in the mould of traditional hymnody), can itself mean a wide variety of items — the Sankey chorus, the contributions of the charismatic movement, the folk-songs that in recent years have come from the Iona Community, and the Taizé music that has won favour in many churches — to name but some.

For the use of this music in church, I want to advance two arguments, and then to offer two criticisms.

(1) Arguments 'for'

Firstly, for many people this style of music is a 'way in' to Christian worship. Easily memorised words, catchy tunes — all these can be a means of worship, an affirmation of the Gospel that speaks to people who are inhibited both by the large tomes which we offer them when they come to church, and by the totally different style of music to which we expect them to adapt.

Secondly, it bears effective witness to the truth that worship involves more than the mind, but brings in our emotions and our bodies, that it helps us to *feel* as well as to think, that it enables us to enjoy what we are doing.

(2) Arguments 'against'

In criticism of it, I would say, firstly that it can unwittingly discourage growth, and keep us in one place when we ought to be moving on. The very fact that it is easy and undemanding can mean that there are some who want to stay with it, and are unwilling to be stretched or enlarged.

Secondly, that the considerable, if not exclusive use of songs can mean that we miss the dimensions of worship that are offered by hymn-writers and composers of many centuries and traditions. This would leave us as much prisoners of a particular culture as those whose praise was limited to Victorian hymns or even those of Charles Wesley.

These two criticisms apply only if the song becomes that which is most prevalent in our worship. When it is popular, there is a real danger that it will take over — to the exclusion of much else. Much as we value mint for many purposes, we do not want our gardens to contain nothing else.

But I believe that this style of music can enrich our worship, bring some fresh air into it and make it more accessible to those who are unfamiliar with traditional liturgy or who have been put off by it. Probably in our larger churches we need two groups of musicians — one which is more traditional, and the other which is more experimental. And we must also remember that hymnody which we have been calling 'traditional' is by no means static, but is itself growing. Had it been otherwise, there would have been no need for the supplements of the 1970s or the *new* standard collections of the 1980s.

Given the validity of these points, it is unlikely that the contents of any one hymn-book will be sufficient for all the needs of the people. It is certainly good to make full use of what we already have in a hymn book. Many Churches do not get the best out of their books because they have not taken the trouble to get to know those books properly. But to be adding regularly to the repertoire of hymns — either from within the book or from outside it — is surely a sign of growth in any congregation.

E. Choosing a 'standard' hymn-book

We are still left with the question of how to choose a standard hymn-book. It would be a pity if this were decided solely by the cost and size of the books or even by the predilections of a prospective donor. And it is somewhat short-sighted to make a choice simply on the grounds of which known items have been included and which left out. Perhaps the matter can best be approached by applying to it the four purposes of hymnody which were suggested in the first chapter.

(1) Congregational participation

Which hymn-book will best enable the participation of the congregation? Here the size, character and capabilities of the congregation will have to be borne in mind, and the question of whether there is a choir and how capable is the instrumentalist. The pitch of the tunes is important here, though there is less divergence in modern hymn books than there was, for example, between the Old Standard and the Revised A & M. The possibility of buying copies of the melody edition for the congregation should certainly be explored; experience shows that this facilitates their participation very considerably, and is well worth the rather greater outlay. Someone will need to do some hard work on the tunes to assess how easily the new ones can be learned. This is often hard to estimate; whether or not a tune will 'go' cannot always be judged until it has actually been tried out.

(2) Doctrinal content

Which hymn-book best represents the doctrines of the Christian Faith? Here we must examine the way in which doctrines are presented, and ask whether this presentation will help people both to understand such doctrines and to make them their own. In this connection it is worth examining the hymns on the Holy Spirit — often feebly represented in older collections, and those which speak of eternal life — somewhat underplayed in some modern hymn-books.

(3) Reality of experience

Which hymn-book will help people to express their experience in what they sing? We must ask whether there are enough hymns that will be 'real' for most of the congregation? Conversely, is there enough material to stretch people and to encourage spiritual growth rather than stagnation? In this, as in the last two considerations, it is important to think not only of the existing congregation, but of those who might join it as the Church continues its mission.

(4) Liturgical appropriateness

Which hymn-book will best meet the liturgical needs of the Church? For which services are hymns regularly required? Is the worship primarily eucharistic, or does it include non-sacramental services? What kind of family worship must be catered for? Is hymnody confined to Sundays? Does the ecumenical situation involve regular shared worship with another congregation and should this mean some joint consultation on the matter? The question of regularity is important here, because it is an expensive luxury to have too many hymns that can be sung only once a year; it is a luxury that must sometimes be afforded — especially when we think of the magnificent hymnody for Palm Sunday! But some collections have, for example, too large a selection for Christmas; this is a time when special carol sheets or duplicated orders of service are often used for the congregation, and the hymn-book itself for only one or two services during the Christmas season.

F. Compiling your own hymn-book

There are, on offer, one or two alternatives to the daunting business of choosing a hymn book. One publishing firm offers the possibility of compiling your own hymn-book, and this sounds attractive. But it could be more limiting than it seems; a balanced selection would require a pretty skilled committee, and the result could be a cause of perennial dissatisfaction. Again there are those who would dispose of books altogether, and recommend the use of a screen and projector. They point out that most people are not used to handling large books and can feel intimidated by them, whereas the majority of people are more accustomed to watching a screen than to reading a book — much less to finding places quickly in it. There are occasions and places where this would work very well — a particular kind of 'guest service' or some act or worship where the emphasis was primarily on the visual. But if, as the final chapter will suggest, hymns are also a means of personal growth and nurture, it is important that people have in their homes the hymn-books they use in church — as well as service books and Bible.

There is more mileage in the idea of creating your own supplement. Again, this requires a fair amount of skill and a large amount of work, but it has been successfully achieved in some communities. The question of copyright is involved here, since the hymns required for such a supplement would be likely to be newer with words and tunes under copyright. Most hymn-books provide clear directions as to where permission to reproduce texts or tunes must be sought, so this merely means a lot of work for both secretary and treasurer.

I have deliberately, and perhaps irritatingly, refrained from offering descriptions or assessments of hymn-books currently in print, and for this there are three reasons. Firstly, to do justice to the broad range of hymn-books available across the various denominations would demand a very wide survey, and a much larger book than this present one. Secondly, any such survey would be quickly out of date, since new hymn-books continue to appear on the market, and reference has already been made to two denominational collections which are, at the time of writing, being made. Thirdly, there is no ready-made answer that can be applied to any community or church, and it is important that questions are asked and research undertaken before a decision is made about the purchase of hymn-books. If I were cast on the proverbial desert island, I think I know which hymn-book I would take with me, but I also know that there are many omissions from it that I would greatly miss.

But the good use of hymns does not depend solely on the material available, and it is only the bad workman who is for ever blaming his tools. A hymn-book with glaring deficiencies can still be used to the greatest advantage, and a fine hymn-book misused through ignorance, negligence and our own deliberate fault. How to make the best use of our books will be the subject of succeeding chapters.

NOTES

1.   This was the title provided for me when asked to write the RSCM Handbook no. 6.

III. CHOOSING THE HYMNS

A. What usually happens?

Tidy churches are no doubt admirable, but it is always disappointing when the hymn-boards are empty or taken down. An Anglican hymn board provides opportunities for endless speculation, and raises questions that seldom get answers. Who chose those hymns? Was it the Minister or the organist, or did two or three get together in the vestry to pick them? Are they the same as they were on the corresponding Sunday last year? What *was* the theme of the service when the selection seems so haphazard?

In the Church of England there is a long tradition of casualness about the selection of hymns. As we have seen, in the two centuries that followed the Reformation, it was often the clerk who determined what part of the metrical psalter should be used. Reginald Heber was one of the most gifted and certainly one of the most lyrical of Anglican hymn-writers. In his preface to hymns published in the *Christian Observer* in 1812, he wrote:

> *The following hymns are part of an intended series, appropriate to the Sundays and principal holy days of the year, connected in some degree with their particular Collects and Gospels, and designed to be sung between the Nicene Creed and the sermon. The effect of an arrangement of this kind, though only partially adopted, is very striking in the Romish liturgy; and its place should seem to be imperfectly supplied by a few verses of the Psalms, entirely unconnected with the peculiar devotions of the day, and selected at the discretion of the clerk.* [1]

There are many different ways in which hymns are chosen nowadays. Sometimes it is the parish priest who makes the choice; sometimes the organist; sometimes a designated member of the congregation. It can be a last-minute business; or hymns may be chosen a month or more ahead. The latter gives the organist and choir time to see what is 'coming up', but often the concealed reason is getting the job out of the way. Only rarely is the preacher involved in the choice — even if he or she is on the parish strength. In few parishes does anyone think it necessary to ask a visiting preacher to contribute ideas. For this reason it is sheer accident if the particular slant given to the ministry of the word is in any way reflected in the hymns. So, however admirable the choice may be in some respects, it is lacking in precision.

It is usually otherwise in the Free Churches.[2] The preacher is generally responsible for the choice of the hymns and for the planning of the service in which they are set. There are, of course, exceptions — requests for particular hymns, or one chosen by the children. A student once found in the vestry a scrap of paper with five numbers on it and the inscription 'these are known'. Now although this method can ensure a proper relationship between preaching and praise, it has the disadvantage that it inevitably can cause too much repetition — especially in those churches where there is a different preacher each Sunday. A congregation can find itself singing *Jesus is Lord* or whatever may be the current craze, for six Sundays running! Odder things can happen. A preacher chose one of the more obscure hymns from the 1933 *Methodist Hymn Book* — *None is Like Jeshurun's God;* he remarked in the vestry that he supposed it was a long time since they had sung this hymn — only to be told 'we had it last Sunday'.

B. What should happen?

In some congregations there is a worship committee, one of whose duties is to plan the selection of hymns. There may be certain occasions where it is desirable for the committee to choose all the hymns for a particular service, but this is likely to be too cumbrous a process to be undertaken on a regular basis. A worship committee can more usefully make a detailed study of its hymn-book, and, in particular, draw up lists of hymns which they think should sometime be sung. This is useful for the selectors, and enables them to feed in such items one by one.

In general, I believe that the final choice of hymns should be the responsibility of one person. In my earlier book *These Are The Hymns*, I argued very strongly that in Anglican churches, this should be the responsibility of the parish priest, or the person leading the worship. I made this point because it is essential that the selectors should have an overall knowledge of the congregation and its needs — young and old, musical and non-musical, and because the selectors must have a clear and precise knowledge of how the worship is to be conducted and how the theme of the day is to be explored. I would now modify this judgment, because there may be others whose skill in the matter is greater than that of the parish priest. It is as important as ever that the person making the choice should have a good knowledge of the needs and capabilities of the congregation.

It is no less important that two other people should be consulted.

The first is the preacher. It is, as we have seen, unnecessary to say this to Free Church people, but very necessary to say it to Anglicans. The way in which both these traditions use hymns is governed by their respective understandings of the place hymns have in worship. But part of the effectiveness of hymns lies in their function as a sort of commentary on Scripture, and as a means by which the congregation can respond to what it has heard. Therefore the preacher should be invited either to suggest a couple of hymns related to his sermon, or to give some account of the theme which he/she intends to pursue. If this makes the preacher work a bit more in advance, it will be to the advantage of the sermon, and the congregation which listens to it.

The second is the organist. As we have seen, the choice is sometimes left to the organist on the grounds that hymns are a musical matter. So they are; but they are also a matter of liturgy, a vehicle of devotion, a subtle form of instruction. It could be argued that the organist should have sole choice of the tunes, and usually there is no one better qualified to make decisions about them. But, again, this arrangement may not be invariable. The organist may be too timid to introduce anything that might be too controversial, or too insensitive to the congregation as a whole, or not very interested anyway in this part of the music. The highly-qualified organist with a good choir may be largely and primarily interested in the choral items, regard hymn-singing as a concession to the less musical, and be prepared to endure anything in that area for the sake of peace and quietness.

However the selection is made, it demands careful planning. Only in this way can a balanced act of worship be secured, and the hymns play that creative role in liturgy which is surely part of their function. Only thus can we avoid those squalid little squabbles that occur in vestries or after services; they nearly always arise from lack of communication and proper understanding of the particular roles of different people involved in leading worship.

C. How to choose: basic principles

We move to some basic considerations about the actual process of choosing hymns.

(1) Liturgical appropriateness

Hymns must be appropriate to the liturgy for which they are chosen. At all points in liturgy for which hymns are chosen, we must ask what is the function of the hymn. Hymns can be ornaments to liturgy or impediments to it. They can facilitate what is happening, or they can interrupt and distract from what is happening. In subsequent chapters, we shall be looking at various kinds of liturgy, and so at the hymnody required for them. Here we make only the general point about liturgical appropriateness, and a general illustration will serve. Anglicans planning some major occasion are apt to end services with something like *O worship the King* — especially if collections are to be taken, or flags returned. This gives everybody a good rousing sing, and lets them go out feeling that they have taken part in a fairly undemanding activity. But is this the way in which a service should end? Should it not culminate in some act of commitment to the service of God and other people? Isaiah 6: 1-8 can serve as a model here. The prophet's story began with the worship of God in the temple, but it did not end there. The conclusion of the story is 'Here I am; send me'.

(2) Thematic appropriateness

Hymns must be appropriate to the theme of the particular Sunday or occasion for which they are chosen. There is substantial similarity between the suggested or prescribed lectionaries of the main-stream churches and each Sunday has a general theme. This must be reflected in the hymns, but not spelt out in each one, for, if it is, the result can be monotonous. An example is Pentecost 7 where the theme is 'the more excellent way'. If the hymns chosen included *Come down O love divine, Love divine all loves excelling* and *O thou who camest from above,* three of them would be saying very much the same thing. The reference to the theme needs to be more indirect and allusive. Moreover, the preacher may, as we shall see, take some theme within a theme, and the manner in which the ministry of the word is interpreted requires its proper reflection in the hymns.

(3) Metrical variety

There needs to be a variety in the metre of the hymns. I once attended a service in which all the hymns (and there were no less than five of them) were in the short metre. I found myself wondering whether this was by design or accident or simply a joke. Since it was a Eucharist largely attended by the Mothers' Union, it seemed unlikely to be the last. If there are four hymns in the service, not more than two should be in the same metre, and ideally all should be of different metre. This is again to avoid monotony — which will be felt by the congregation, though not all will discern its cause.

(4) Variety of sources

For the same reason, there should be variety in the periods of history to which both texts and tunes belong. It is undesirable that all the music should be by John Bacchus Dykes or by Orlando Gibbons. It is also desirable that the texts should come from different centuries, and if this apparently minor consideration is borne in mind, it will again ensure some variety in the worship.

(5) Balance between 'old' and 'new'

There must be a reasonable balance between what is 'new' and what is 'old' or, more accurately, between what is 'known' and what is 'not known'. (Some people will, of course, describe the *Old 124th* as a 'new' tune if they do not happen to know it). This matter, as already suggested, is not easy to determine. What is known to the person who attends church on most Sundays is different from what is known to someone who comes two or three times a year. A person with a reasonable musical ear will know a hymn when it has been sung a couple of times, whereas an unmusical person may still find it new when it has been sung half a dozen times. The person who chooses hymns needs — if it is possible — both sensitivity to the congregation and a fairly thick skin in view of the criticisms likely to be received.

There is no way of avoiding the remark 'we didn't know that hymn', even if the repertoire is limited to fifty. But there are ways of ensuring that you do not hear it too often. When something quite new is chosen, the remaining hymns should be very well-known; and if four hymns are sung, not more than two should be lesser-known. It is essential to ensure that *some* people know the tune and will give a good lead — to avoid the most damning criticism of all ('nobody knew the tune'). Past hymn-lists will indicate when a hymn was last sung and at which service. Future pages in this book will say something about the introduction of 'new' hymns.

(6) Avoiding repetition

Care should be taken to avoid too much repetition of the same hymns. Sometimes, in the case of a new hymn, it is worth singing it (if possible) on one or two Sundays close together in order to get it known. But it is sad to see hymns so overworked that people grow tired of singing them. *Praise my soul* is an example from older hymnody, and *We have a gospel to proclaim* from newer collections. Among tunes, *Slane* is set to too many contemporary hymns (there are good alternatives if people will learn them) and the fine tune *Westminster Abbey* is all too predictable on grand occasions.

A simple method of avoiding too much repetition is to have a note-book in which the numbers of the hymns are set out line by line. Against it you enter the date on which the hymn was sung. It may be necessary to add the letters M or E if the church has both morning and evening services; for when the congregations are largely different, a hymn sung in the morning can be repeated in the evening a week or two later. This can be applied particularly to seasons like Advent or Easter. Apart from revealing what hymns were sung when, it will also indicate which hymns are never sung. For their total omission, there may be the best of reasons; but there may also be some hymns that have just been overlooked and deserve more of an airing than they get.

D. Helps in Choosing

So far this chapter has set out the task that awaits selectors of hymns if they are to do the job well. We go on to suggest ways in which they can be helped to fulfil it.

First, there is no substitute for a thorough knowledge of the contents of the hymn-book in use. In 1982, a commentary on *With One Voice* was published with the title *Songs of the People of God*. In a pungent introduction, Wesley Milgate outlined the obligations of clergy, organists and congregation. For the latter he said:

> The first obligation of a congregation, when the use of a new hymn-book is begun, is to read through the contents of the book including the preface; its musical members should also play the music through.[3]

But he added '*needless to say, these duties are practically never undertaken*'. Nor are the obligations of clergy and organists always fully undertaken.

Nevertheless it is essential that those who select hymns should be thoroughly familiar with their books. They need to take note, too, of the manner in which hymn-books are set out, since the arrangement of a hymn-book gives some clue as to how the editors believe it should be used. Moreover, the arrangement imposes itself almost sub-consciously on those who use the book.

Most Anglican collections are arranged *liturgically*. As we have seen, hymns in the Anglican tradition have generally and understandably been seen as accompaniments to the liturgy already provided, and one famous Victorian collection had the revealing title *Hymnal Companion to the Book of Common Prayer*. Among contemporary collections, the *New English Hymnal* is, like the parent volume, an example of the liturgical arrangement. The hymns begin with the Christian Year, cover some other times and seasons, and have a section on sacraments and other rites; the title 'General Hymns' is still used for a large number of the hymns, and 'Church and People' for the rest of them. The hymn-book of the Church of Scotland (*Church Hymnary*, Third edition) is, by contrast *doctrinal* in its emphasis. The first three sections have the titles:

Approach to God
The Word of God: His mighty acts
Response to the Word of God

with various sub-divisions under each. Wesley's 1780 collection was arranged according to *experience*. It began by 'exhorting sinners to return to God' and went on to provide hymns for believers rejoicing, praying, watching and so forth. This sort of method has been used by various evangelical collections. An interesting attempt, suggested by Erik Routley, was made by the Reformed Church in America to create a hymn-book[4] which was arranged *biblically*. Here the hymns begin with creation (Genesis) and end with the triumph of God and his Kingdom (Revelation). Many hymn-books have a classification which is a mixture of these things, and some, for example, *Hymns Old and New*, set out their contents simply in alphabetical order.

All this is mentioned for two reasons. First, the manner in which the hymn-book is arranged will be of help to those who seek to choose hymns for the tradition of the Church for which it is intended. But secondly, it is important to remember that the way in which hymns are classified has usually been determined by the editors of the book, and need not be binding upon those who use it. For example, *Hail to the Lord's anointed* is appointed in some collections as an 'Epiphany' hymn. For that season it is highly appropriate, but this does not mean that there are no other occasions for which it is equally appropriate. These include missionary gatherings, sermons on the kingdom of God, and after the opening sentence for the eighth Sunday before Easter in the ASB. *Stupendous height of heavenly love* was classified under 'Incarnation' in the 1933 *Methodist Hymn Book;* in *Hymns and Psalms* it comes under 'People of the Light', but could equally well find itself in some section that was concerned with death and eternal life.

Of course many hymn books end each section with a list of other hymns suitable for it. It is also worth while for those who choose hymns to annotate their own books, making a brief note of occasions when the hymn has been found suitable. But for further help, we need to turn to the back of our hymn books. Most collections published since the adoption by the churches of a common lectionary have lists of hymns related to the theme of the day, and there are guides to the way in which that theme is represented in various hymn books.[5] Lists of hymns for all the services on a Sunday are printed in some Anglican collections like the *New English Hymnal*; this does no more than ensure a widespread coverage of the book and a certain liturgical appropriateness. Some hymn-books have a scriptural index; the *Anglican Hymn Book* is one example, and the full music edition of *Hymns and Psalms* another; this enables the reader to see how a particular text or passage is interpreted in hymnody. Other collections like *Hymns for Today* (whether in its separate version or as it is included in AMNS) have a subject-index for their contents.

The last is an outstanding feature of *Companion to Hymns and Psalms* published in 1988.[6] This follows a tradition in Methodism which has facilitated the skilful use of hymns by its preachers. The 1988 Companion has several large pages of subject-index with no less than three on aspects of our Lord's nature and ministry. Those who do not use this hymn-book would still find this subject-index useful, since, on many themes, it would suggest use of hymns from their own book that might otherwise escape notice.

A companion or commentary to a hymn-book is of great value to those who choose hymns. For they will surely be interested enough in the subject to want to know more about the hymns which they choose — and sometimes about those which they reject or ignore. Such companions are also invaluable in drawing up a hymn festival, or for preachers who want to talk about a particular hymn. Various studies of popular hymns are available, but full companions to hymn-books tend to go quickly out of print as the books themselves age.

E. Why bother?

The task outlined in this chapter probably seems formidable. Some readers are doubtless wondering whether all this trouble is worthwhile. There is no tangible evidence that the careful choice of hymns affects the spiritual quality of the congregation, much less its size. Many people will not notice whether the hymn seems appropriate or not; their sole concern is whether they know it or like it. Time is precious; can it, ought it to be spent in this way?

Against arguments of this kind, there are three things to be said:

Firstly, if a congregation is gradually educated in hymnody, it will gradually appreciate its use in church. At least, some members will become aware of its importance. They will not need to know all the details that go into the planning of worship, but they will come to realise that it holds together, and builds them up. I take my car to be serviced because I do not have the time or skill to do it myself; I do not need to know all that went on at the garage — I merely know whether or not the car is running well.

Secondly, in every congregation there are various callings, various ministries to be fulfilled. Choosing hymns is one of them — alongside lay visiting or editing the magazine. Can the choice of hymns be of less importance, for example, than flower-arranging to which some people give much time and skill?

Thirdly, as I suggested in my book *Interpreting Worship*[7], the time and trouble taken over its details could be a modern application of those interminable chapters in the Old Testament that deal with the sanctuary and its furnishings. Again, if we know anything of what goes into the making of a television or radio programme, there are lessons to be learned about preparation for the worship of God.

NOTES

1. Quoted by Bernard Braley, *Hymnwriters I* (Stainer and Bell, 1987), p. 69.
2. Doddridge wrote hymns to follow the sermon and appended the text.
3. Milgate, *Songs of the People of God* (Collins, 1982), p. 14.
4. *Rejoice in the Lord* (Eerdmans, 1985).
5. See Robin Leaver, *Hymns for the New Lectionary* (Grove Books, 1980); *A Hymn Guide* (Mowbrays, 1981); Alan Dunstan and Martin Ellis, *Companion to the Lectionary, Vol. 2; Hymns and Anthems* (Epworth, 1983). The last of these is concerned with Anglican and Methodist hymn-books. In 1976 St Andrew's Press produced *A Year's Praise* for use with the *Church Hymnary, 3rd edition*. Darby, *Choosing the Hymns* (Collins, 1984) is a very detailed handbook suggesting hymns on all Scriptural passages provided in the alternative Sunday Lectionary of the Church of Ireland.
6. Watson and Trickett (ed.), *Companion to Hymns and Psalms* (Methodist Publishing House, 1988).
7. Alan Dunstan, *Interpreting Worship* (Mowbrays, 1984).

IV. HYMNS AT THE EUCHARIST

A. Emergence of a common eucharistic framework

A remarkable development in recent church history has been the emergence of a common framework for the Eucharist. This is discernible in the printed orders of service for the Church of England, the Church of Scotland, and the Methodist, United Reformed and Roman Catholic Churches. The situation in the Church of England is reflected in the liturgies of the Anglican Communion, and the documents of the Lima Conference reveal a similar coming together of Churches of many traditions in the matter of eucharistic liturgy. But if we confine ourselves to the churches and service-books mentioned above (i.e. C. of E., C. of S., Methodist, U.R.C. and R.C.) a clear pattern is seen to emerge. In these eucharistic orders there is:

1. a form of preparation which includes an act of praise, some form of approach, and usually a corporate expression of penitence.
2. a ministry of the word, consisting of two or three readings from the Bible, a sermon in close association with them and often the recitation of a creed.
3. a variable form of intercession.
4. the commonly-accepted four-fold action (taking, thanking, breaking, sharing):
   (a) an offertory or setting of the table, (b) a eucharistic prayer usually including the institution narrative unless this is read separately, (c) the breaking of bread and (d) the communion.
5. a brief concluding rite culminating in the dismissal.

Whatever their differences of understanding or practice, this general structure is common to all the rites that we are considering.

Of course the situation is not quite as simple as this may sound. The Book of Common Prayer remains on the statute book as the norm of Anglican worship, and many parishes have some, if not all, celebrations of Holy Communion according to this pattern, which now begins to look rather strange and insular. The Methodists have in their service book the 1936 order of Holy Communion closely modelled on 1662. In the non-episcopalian churches of these islands, the service-books do not have the same authority as they hold in the Roman Catholic and Anglican churches; often they are used more as source-books for liturgy than as providing precise orders of worship. Nevertheless the structure outlined above is generally and increasingly being accepted as 'normal'. All this is a remarkable development in the Church of England itself; half a century ago it seemed that the bitter controversies attending the proposed revision of the Prayer Book in 1927 and 1928 were irreconcilable. It is even more remarkable when the situation before the Second Vatican Council is recalled; the difference between the Latin Mass with few communicants and the communion seasons of the Kirk then seemed hardly bridgeable.

B. The Liturgical use of hymns within this framework

The service books to which I have referred all make provision for hymnody. Again, there is great similarity in the positions assigned to hymns in the liturgy. Four places for hymns are common to these rites:

1. a hymn very near the beginning of the service.
2. the possibility of hymnody between the readings. Psalms and canticles are sometimes offered as alternatives and sometimes required. In the ASB, a psalm is the only permitted link between the Old and New Testament readings, whereas a psalm, canticle or hymn may be sung between the New Testament reading and the Gospel. The Roman Catholic order provides for a responsorial psalm after the first reading, and for the 'Alleluia' before the Gospel, a sung acclamation to greet the Gospel.
3. a hymn before the eucharistic action begins. This may be sung during the collection of money or the offering of the elements, or these activities may precede or follow the hymn.
4. a hymn sung directly after communion or before the blessing or dismissal.

There are other possibilities for hymnody in these rites. A rubric in the ASB makes clear that although positions for hymns are indicated, they may occur elsewhere if occasion requires. The Methodists suggest that a hymn may be sung in place of the *Gloria in excelsis:* if used at that point, it would come hard on the heels of the first hymn. The URC order does not include a creed in the service, but proposes a hymn directly after the sermon. Hymns during the administration of Communion are suggested both in the Anglican and Roman Catholic orders. The 'index of uses' in the Roman Catholic *Celebration Hymnal* includes hymns appropriate to the 'Peace' with the implication that they are sometimes sung at this point.

So we turn to a more detailed consideration of the kinds of hymns required for these positions in the liturgy.

(1) The opening hymn (sometimes called Introit or Entrance Song)

This is not usually a difficult hymn to choose. Indeed, there are festivals where it chooses itself. There is a good selection of classical hymns that are suitable for the beginning of worship, and a few newly-written that can be sung here. The mood is generally that of praise and adoration, though an invocation of the Holy Spirit is no less appropriate.

In many traditions the service opens with a sentence of Scripture. The ASB has offered a 'proper' sentence for each Sunday and festival of the year. When a hymn follows, it ought to be in some way connected with the sentence, unless the latter is to be left suspended in mid-air. It looks as if some of these sentences were rather hastily selected; some, indeed, set the theme of the day without being, in any way, a call to worship. 'Be subject for the Lord's sake to every human institution' (Pentecost 15) is a bald and rather chilling introduction, and it is hard to find any hymn that would be both related to it and a fitting 'entrance song'. 'Abraham is the father of all: as Scripture says, I have made you the father of many nations' (7 before Christmas) is a rather obscure text suggesting for most congregations *The God of Abraham praise* as the only known hymn related to it. But you might not want to be stuck with this fine hymn as the invariable introit on this Sunday, and if the sermon were to be about Abraham, it might be used more suitably as the offertory hymn. Alternative courses for Anglicans are therefore (a) to omit the sentence on occasions when it does not seem to be appropriate; it is not mandatory; (b) to use one of the introductory sentences suggested on pp 37-43 of the ASB. These are printed before the orders of Morning and Evening Prayer, but the rubric makes clear that they may also be used at Holy Communion; (c) to select another sentence for the particular occasion. It would hardly be a serious breach of discipline if the president/preacher were sometimes to do this. The Roman Catholic and Methodist orders do not offer sentences at this point, though they are sometimes used in the latter, and the Church of Scotland and United Reformed orders make clear that the printed sentences are only suggestions of what might be read.

This is not usually considered the best place in the service for the introduction of a new tune. Nevertheless if the new hymn/tune falls most naturally at the beginning of worship, a short practice might take place as people are gathering. Indeed, this is, in many places, a good time for the learning of new hymns. It is as worthy an activity as the buzz (or roar) of conversation that is so often a prelude to worship, and as good a preparation for it as discussion about next year's holiday or this Sunday's dinner. In turn, the practice could be followed by a time of corporate silence before the worship itself begins.

(2) The hymn between the readings (sometimes called Gradual)

When a hymn is sung between readings, it is obviously intended to serve as a link between them. In the BCP there was often very little connection between the Epistle and Gospel, whereas the readings in the new lectionary are bound by a general theme. The various lists of hymns appropriate to a particular Sunday theme will be of help here. Also of considerable value are the indexes of Scriptural hymns now included in some hymn-books and recommended in the last chapter.

This is also a suitable place for hymns on the Scriptures as a whole. Not surprisingly, perhaps, Free Church hymnals have generally offered a wider selection of hymns on the Scriptures than their Anglican counterparts, but modern collections of every tradition tend to increase the number of hymns on the Bible — probably with this liturgical need in mind. A meditation on the Scriptures can be very appropriate at this stage. But it is, perhaps a little odd to sing a hymn asking for help and illumination in understanding the Scriptures when the more difficult part of them has already been heard. Congregations do not consist of New Testament critics, and most people find the Gospel passage easier to understand than the others. However, this point may seem over-precise. But I would suggest that very occasionally, and by way of variety, a hymn asking for help in reading the Scriptures might be sung before any part of them is read (in the Anglican order this would follow the Collect) and the passages themselves might then be followed by a period of silence.

As we have noted, the Roman Catholic order provides for the 'Alleluia' or 'Gospel Acclamation' for which there is ancient precedent. It is outside the scope of this book to discuss the wider use of such a chant before the Gospel; it is just within its scope to suggest the provision of metrical (i.e. hymn) forms of the Gospel Acclamation. This could be a new field for hymn-writers.

(3) The hymn before the eucharistic action

This is the most difficult of the four hymns to choose, and much depends upon what its function is seen to be. The rubric in the Missal runs:

> At the beginning of the liturgy of the eucharist, the gifts which will become the Lord's body and blood are brought to the altar. The offerings of the people may also be brought to the altar. During the procession of gifts, the people may sing an offertory song.

The ASB has the rubric — rather confusingly placed — 'at the preparation of the gifts a hymn may be sung', and the URC order says it 'may be sung while the money, bread and wine are brought to the Table'. The *Book of Common Order* (1979) uses the phrase 'the Great Entrance' and one of its three orders suggests the traditional *Ye gates, lift up your heads* or another suitable psalm or hymn.

The hymn at this point could be a simple commentary on what is happening, though most hymns under the title 'offertory' go on to point the moral of self-offering. In 1960, J.A.T. Robinson wrote:

> And in the offertory we are simply taking a dip into the world and lifting out of it a sample of the common livelihood of man — a loaf of bread and a bottle of drink.

He saw bread as a symbol of work, and wine as a symbol of leisure, and went on:

> All that we take, as it were, off the table of our daily lives, and we place it in the hands of Christ for him to transform and use.[1].

This was a common interpretation of 'offertory' during the earlier years of liturgical revision, but was challenged by those who suspected it of Pelagianism. In 1978 came Colin Buchanan's Grove pamphlet *The End of the Offertory,* and this in turn affected the interpretation of the service suggested by the Liturgical Commission in their official commentary in 1980. On this point they write:

> It cannot be too highly stressed that this provision of bread and wine is **not** an integral part of the eucharistic action, but only a preliminary to it.[2].

And they see the first eucharistic action (the taking) not in the bringing up of the elements nor in the placing of them on the altar, but in the action required in section 36 of Rite A — the taking:

> *The president takes the bread and cup into his hands and replaces them on the holy table.*

This is a rubric that seems to be commonly ignored, forgotten or mis-understood.

This brief excursion into recent Anglican liturgical history is made in order to help us answer the question of what sort of hymn is appropriate at this stage in the service. Clearly, there are those who, for theological reasons, would not want a hymn of self-offering at this point; and if, as I shall argue, dedication ought to be the note of the final hymn in the service, there could be duplication and confusion at this point. If the hymn is accompanying actions that are *preparatory* to the eucharistic action, it is arguably still part of the ministry of the Word, or at least a link between that part of the service and the ministry of the sacrament. In most of the orders we have considered, it is the first hymn to be sung after the sermon, although in the Anglican order it is separated from it by creed, intercessions and perhaps the prayers of penitence. Nevertheless, it could be regarded as the hymn most closely related to the sermon; and it will be equally appropriate before the eucharistic action if the sermon itself points to those mighty acts of God which will be recited in the eucharistic prayer.

It is, however, questionable whether a hymn ought to be sung at all whilst other activities are in progress. If the offering of money is an integral part of worship, should it be 'covered up' in this way? Or if the placing of elements on the Holy Table is still seen as a significant liturgical action, does it not deserve the attention of worshippers? Apart from these considerations, we must think of the importance we allow to the hymn; can it be sung properly if people are fumbling for coins or envelopes? And what does the chink of money do for the music?

Time is always cited as an important factor here. And maybe for this reason, we must continue singing during what many would regard as rather humdrum activities. But there are other possibilities for the hymn that could be considered:

(a) It could be sung immediately after the intercessions or even after the Peace, but *before* the preparation of the gifts. This would link it more closely with the ministry of the word.

(b) It could be sung after all the collecting and placing on the altar has been done. This would make it more specifically a eucharistic hymn. And since length would no longer be an important consideration, it would make it possible for the whole congregation to sing such short and beautiful texts as *Author of life divine* or *Be known to us in breaking bread.*

(4) The final hymn

Most liturgies suggest a hymn either directly after communion, or immediately after the post-communion prayer, and before the blessing or dismissal. The former is the recommended position in Rite A, and if the post-communion sentence is used, the same considerations that were mentioned in connection with the opening hymn will need to be borne in mind. The URC order suggests the possibility of a doxology. But what should be avoided is some general hymn of praise that might equally have been chosen for the beginning of the service. The object of a hymn at this point is not to give the congregation 'a good sing', but to help them understand and express their calling as God's people in His world. This is not usually the moment to recount the mighty acts of God which have been recalled at various times in the liturgy, and notably in the eucharistic prayer. The concluding rites of contemporary liturgies are invariably brief, and very much concered with the theme of dismissal for service, and all that remains is to go in peace to love and serve the Lord.

An element of thanksgiving (which is subtly different from praise) is appropriate here, but the main thrust of the hymn must surely be the inescapable connection between worship and mission. A fair number of good modern hymns have been written with this specific purpose in mind. The days are long past when the magnificent *Forth in thy name* seemed the only alternative to the post-communion hymns from ancient liturgies. And a reasonable knowledge of any hymn-book will extend the range of possibilities to what is well beyond the immediately obvious.

(5) Other places for hymnody

(a) during communion

It is suggested in both the Anglican and Roman Catholic orders that hymns may be sung during the administration of communion. But the great eucharistic hymns of the Wesleys were sung during the prolonged administration at communion services during the revival. Modern preference is usually for quiet and devotional hymnody, especially if the choir is situated between the people and the altar. At a long administration, the alternation of choral and instrumental music seems preferable to continuous singing; and if both kinds of music are interspersed with silence, their impact is heightened.

(b) processions

The formal or special procession is discussed in another chapter. The desirability of a hymn during the entrance and exit of the choir must depend somewhat on the choreography of the building, but the question of what its effect is intended to be needs to be considered. People sometimes speak of a hymn 'to get the choir out' as if it were incapable of moving without choral accompaniment. It is simply worth asking what such processions are saying (a) about the liturgy and (b) about the choir.

(c) Methodist/URC variants

We have noted that in the Methodist order, a hymn may be sung in place of the *Gloria;* presumably its content would be similar, though expressed in a different form. The URC direction of a hymn immediately after the sermon provides an opportunity for one that is directly related to it. Anglicans might consider such a possibility on those rare occasions when the Nicene Creed is not mandatory.

(d) variety of positions

Alternative positions for hymns have been suggested a number of times in these last few pages. Most Anglicans (and probably many others) expect hymns to be sung at certain fixed points in the liturgy. And for forty Sundays in the year, this is probably right. But perhaps once a month — or less — there is a case for singing hymns at other than the conventional points. The advantages are:
(i) that the congregation may attend to its hymnody rather more carefully if there is a special reason for changing the position
(ii) that it will enable a special kind of hymn to be sung at a place appropriate to it
(iii) it is a response to that flexibility and variety that are built into most modern liturgies. 'We always have a hymn at this stage' is not a cast-iron reason for having one.

(e) practices to be avoided

(i) There are churches where part of a hymn is sung before the Gospel, and part at its conclusion. This could have its uses if the hymn were specially written for the purpose; but very few English hymns lend themselves to such treatment. A careful selection of verses is often highly desirable, but if the last verse is always lopped off for use later in the service, the effect on the hymn is usually disastrous.

(ii) A dismissal such as 'Go in peace to love and serve the Lord' with congregational response is mandatory in most liturgies, and such words are meant to be the *final* words of the service. Their significance is totally missed if a hymn then follows. If both blessing and dismissal are used, a hymn may be sung between the two if necessity so requires, but the dismissal must be *last* if it is to have real meaning and force. I have myself written often about this, and am gratified that the same point is made very strongly in a book by the former Director of the Royal School of Church Music.[3]

C. Thematic Hymns at the Eucharist

We have so far considered the kinds of hymns required for various points in the liturgy. But the liturgy itself is given a different character Sunday by Sunday by reason of its variable content — most notably, the readings appointed in the ministry of the word. Since the publication and widespread adoption of the calendar and eucharistic lectionary originally proposed by the Joint Liturgical Group, each Sunday has had a general theme, but it has been urged more than once that the themes are no more than general indicators, and should not be allowed to dictate the use of the scriptural material. In the ASB, the themes are listed towards the end of the book and the 1980 commentary ran:

> *It cannot be too strongly emphasised that scripture is primary and must be allowed to speak for itself, while the themes set out in the tables are secondary and provided only as 'guides for those who wish to use them'. In framing the table of readings the passages from the Bible which ought to be read were first selected, and only then were they ordered and given sequence so that some general progression of theme emerged. The Joint Liturgical Group insisted that the thematic titles are no more than indications of emphasis, and must not be allowed to give false rigidity to the hearing of scripture or the preaching of the Word of God.*[4]

The same point is made in the fuller and more recent commentary on the Alternative Service Book.[5]

The effect of this on hymnody can be illustrated by looking at a random Sunday. We take the twelfth Sunday after Pentecost when the theme is 'the witnessing community'. If that is the preacher's starting-point, and he perhaps intends to range over the various Scriptural passages, there is no lack of hymns on such a theme. Adopting the four 'agreed' positions for hymns, the result might be:

	AMNS	H&P
1. Ye Servants of God	149	278
2. In Christ there is no east or west	376	758
3. Christ is the King!	345	
or See how great a flame		781
4. We have a gospel to proclaim	431	465

But there are other possibilities for the preacher. In Year 1, he might want to expound the servant song from Isaiah 49. From the New Testament lesson, he might take (i) the new order in Christ (2 Cor 5: 14-17) or (ii) the ministry of reconciliation (2 Cor 5: 18-21) or (iii) he might want to focus on the last two verses of the reading (2 Cor 6: 1, 2) with its demand for immediate response to the Gospel. Unity in mission is a subject that might be drawn from the Gospel reading. In Year 2, Micah's vision of a world at peace forms the Old Testament lesson, the reading from Acts raises the question of how the Gospel may be proclaimed in an alien culture, and the symbols of 'light' and 'salt' are the obvious possibilities from the Gospel.

Now the general list above will not contain the best selection for all these subjects. A standard list will not do for this Sunday, and the selection must be made with the particular as well as the general theme in mind. Some hymns may be common to most of the lists we might devise, but some are bound to be different. Suppose in Year 2, it is the Old Testament lesson that grips the preacher, and this is the passage that he wants to expound to the congregation. The list might then be:

	AMNS	H&P
1. Tell out my soul	422	86
2. Christ is the world's true light	346	456
3. We turn to you	522	412
or All glory to God in the Sky		400
4. Praise the Lord, rise up rejoicing	416	
or Make me a channel of your peace		776

The first three hymns are common to the two contemporary hymn-books that I have chosen, but some Methodists might prefer Wesley's *All glory to God in the sky* for the third hymn. They do not have the fine post-communion hymn *Praise the Lord, rise up, rejoicing* and the popular version of what is known as 'St Francis' Prayer' is missing from AMNS.

But suppose the preacher takes a single text for his sermon. It is from the New Testament lesson, and it is Acts 17:32. He talks about three kinds of postponement: (a) the postponement that we must make until we know more about the subject; (b) the postponement in which we hide because we want to evade the implications of making a decision; (c) the postponement that comes about because, although we are full of good intentions, we simply do not 'get around to' the matter. The hymn-list would look rather different from the one in which Micah's vision was the theme, and might be as follows:

	AMNS	H&P
1. Come, let us with our Lord arise	449	575
2. Christ is the world's light, he and none other	440	455
or Thanks be to God		570
3. Dear Lord and Father of mankind	115	673
or Come sinners to the gospel feast		460
4. The kingdom is upon you	512	
or A charge to keep I have		785

The first three hymns are again common to both books. *Come, let us with our Lord arise* says all the right things for an opening hymn, and points to the resurrection which Paul preaches in the passage from Acts. *Christ is the world's light* makes a fitting commentary on the lesson, and is a prelude to *You are the light of the world* in the Gospel. The alternative hymn in H&P is a new composition by Caryl Micklem, and seems to fit the passage like a glove. Note especially verse 2:

Thanks be to God, whose Spirit sent
Apostles out upon his way;
From east to west the message went;
On Greek and Roman dawned the day.

Dear Lord and Father is a popular choice at most times, and its message should be clear in this context. Methodists might prefer a hymn with the verse:

This is the time; no more delay!
This is the Lord's accepted day;
Come in, this moment, at his call,
And live for him who died for all.

though they might hesitate to choose it if *Thanks be to God* had been sung as the preceding hymn, since both are in the long metre. The revisers of AMR dropped *A charge to keep* from their new collection, and had not perhaps had a chance to see the invisible mending which it received in H&P. But they did include *The kingdom is upon you* which would make a good closing hymn for such a day with such a theme.

The 'witnessing community' may seem so general a theme that it permits this diverse treatment. We look at a Sunday where the theme may seem more specific — Christ the Healer. This is the eighth Sunday before Easter and for the general theme there is not a particularly good selection. I will not this time provide the reader with a list of sermon-subjects, but merely note — again in Year 2 — that a sermon on Naaman might suggest different hymnody from one based on the Gospel passage with its stories of the Syro-Phoenician woman and the deaf mute. The first, which will have some reference to 'the scandal of particularity' involved by the river Jordan, might have the following list:

	AMNS	H&P
1. Jesus, where'er thy people meet	162	459
2. O God, by whose almighty plan	406	396
3. Jesu, Lover of my soul	123	528
4. Awake our souls, away our fears	436	663

But the second might be

	AMNS	H&P
1. O for a thousand tongues to sing	125	744
2. Lord Christ, who on thy heart	388	
or Your words to me are life and health		482
3. I heard the voice of Jesus say	247	136
4. Glory, love, and praise, and honour	461	35

The second selection from H&P may be rather academic, for (as with the Church of Scotland) Mark 1: 35-45 is the Gospel on this Sunday. But Mark 7: 24-37 remains an evening lesson in the

Methodist lectionary, and the URC follows the Anglican practice of appointing it as the Gospel.

These are not intended to be ideal lists; such things do not exist. This section of the chapter is designed to show:

(a) that each Sunday requires a fresh list of hymns. It is not enough to look back at last year's list, or even to what was sung two years ago.

(b) that the choice of hymns requires the co-operation of the preacher. It cannot be restricted to people who, though they may have considerable skills in and wide knowledge of hymnody, have no idea of what the preacher's theme will be.

(c) that hymns chosen with such a theme in mind do not have to be all of the same kind, much less to be saying the same thing.

(d) the liturgical and thematic choice of hymns need not be in conflict with each other.

The Roman Catholic lectionary follows a three-year cycle, and although I have not provided illustrations from it, I hope that Roman Catholic readers will be able to make use of the principles set out in this chapter for their own choice of hymns. For the hymn is one means by which the liturgy is constantly renewed, and its power applied to the worshippers.

NOTES

1. John A.T. Robinson, *Liturgy Coming to Life* (Mowbrays, 1960), p. 62.
2. The *Alternative Service Book (1980): a commentary by the Liturgical Commission* (CIO), p. 77.
3. Lionel Dakers *Using and Choosing Hymns* (Mowbrays, 1985) pp. 48-9.
4. *ASB: commentary, op. cit.,* p. 30.
5. R.C.D. Jasper and Paul F. Bradshaw, *A Companion to the Alternative Service Book* (SPCK, 1986), p. 309.

V. HYMNS AT NON-SACRAMENTAL SERVICES

A. Anglican Matins and Evensong

In our discussion of hymns for the Anglican Eucharist, we assumed the 'newer' (but in fact more classical) shape of the liturgy as represented in Rite A and Rite B and as paralleled in many other Churches. For Matins and Evensong, it would be unsafe to do so. Where they survive as choral services, the BCP forms are likely, if not more likely to be found. The ASB forms do not much differ from those of the BCP in shape, but are distinguished by the use of modern language and the provision of alternatives — most notably in the canticles. But the growth of the sort of eucharistic worship often described as 'the parish communion' meant a sharp decline in the use of Matins as a choral service on Sundays. It has also contributed to a similar decline in Sunday Evensong, though social changes are primarily responsible for the mild revolution that has changed evening worship from being the most popular of the day into services usually attended by very small numbers.

Hymns are, of course, as much interlopers in the Prayer Book forms of Matins and Evensong as they were in its order of Holy Communion. But, as we have seen, there was a long tradition of singing metrical psalms before and after the sermon (though, until the middle of the nineteenth century, this would always have been at the ante-Communion), and hymns came to be used in the same places at Matins and Evensong. The 1662 book included the famous rubric 'in quires and places where they sing, here followeth the anthem', and where there was no anthem, a hymn was usually sung also at this point. The popularity of hymns meant that a number of other places in these services was found for them.

In our own time, we can identify certain places in which hymnody is common at these services, and so begin to ask questions about their function. First a hymn is frequently sung at the beginning of Matins and Evensong. Liturgical purists used to object to this on the grounds that the services were meant to open penitentially, and that it was anachronistic to have 'O Lord, open thou our lips' fairly soon after the singing of a rousing hymn. On the first point, it has been argued (again following the pattern of Isaiah 6: 1-8) that we are moved to penitence *after* we have in some way apprehended the holiness and goodness of God. As to the second criticism, it is no more anachronistic than to sing 'The Lord be with you' in the course of a service at which He has surely been already present. The ASB orders suggest the use of a sentence and hymn directly after the call to, and explanation of worship has been made.

Considerations affecting the choice of those hymns are similar to those put forward in the last chapter for the choice of the introit at the Eucharist. In the case of the ASB, the opening sentence is more likely to come from the selection offered on pp. 37-42 of that book, and these sentences are generally related to the season as a whole and not to the theme of a particular Sunday. Those who claim to use the 1662 service often borrow vey considerably from the material offered in the revision fo 1928, and this included sentences relating to the seasons and to worship as a whole rather than to penitence in particular. The hymn that follows such sentences will consequently often be seasonal in character; or it will be a hymn in which the attributes of God in creation, redemption or sanctification are set forth; and in either case it is likely to be a hymn which evokes the adoration of those who have assembled for worship.

The other hymns follow the collects, and the sort of hymns chosen must depend upon the way in which the service is then arranged. Following the 'third collect' at Matins or Evensong, the order could be:
hymn-prayers-hymn-sermon-hymn-blessing;
or it could be:
hymn-sermon-hymn-prayers-hymn-blessing.
The hymns might be reduced in number by the singing of an anthem, or by the putting together of collects and prayers or by the leading of prayers directly after the sermon.

We will consider the first two of these possibilities, and leave the reader to make adjustments if the other options are taken. The hymn in place of the anthem could again be seasonal; or it could be hymn about prayer; or it could be a hymn about the kingdom of God with which the prayers will surely be concerned. The hymn before the sermon would then be a preparation for it. It might introduce the theme of the sermon; or it might be a hymn asking for illumination in our understanding of the scriptures, or it might be an invocation of the Holy Spirit. The hymn that follows the sermon should obviously be closely related to it, and be able to express the response of the congregation to the word of God as it has been preached. My argument that the preacher should be involved in the choice of hymns applies most particularly to what is chosen here. The effect of the sermon can quickly be dissipated if the hymn that immediately follows is totally unrelated to it, or even in some way contradictory to what has been said. *Father, hear the prayer we offer* could hardly follow an exposition of the 23rd Psalm, nor *Light's abode, celestial Salem* a sermon which had focussed on some area of Christian social concern.

If the second arrangement is followed, the same considerations apply to the hymns chosen before and after the sermon. The prayers that follow will themselves be followed by a hymn and the blessing. This should be a simple act of dedication, or if that has already been adequately expressed in the previous hymn, there is a place at Evensong for an evening hymn with which to conclude the service. But, again, it is desirable that the closing hymn of these, as of most other services, should in some way be connected with the service of God which we are to offer when we have left the church.

The ASB orders of Morning and Evening Prayer suggest the possibility of the sermon directly after the second lesson, and this would give to the services a structure rather similar to that of the Eucharistic Liturgy of the word. But it would also mean that the sermon was followed by a canticle which would rarely relate very directly to what had been said. The reflection of the sermon in the hymns would then have to wait until later in the service; it could be made in the hymn before the prayers, but should certainly be made in the closing hymn.

Other positions for hymnody must briefly be considered. Fortunately, the 'recessional hymn' is much less common than it was a quarter of a century ago; when it follows the blessing it greatly weakens the note of 'sending out' which has been struck in the blessing itself — most particularly if the various forms suggested by the ASB are used. With the decline of Evensong as a major service, there is a similar decline in the formal procession that used to follow the office on festivals in churches of a more Catholic tradition. When this is simply a circular walk around the church, the suggestions made by older writers like Percy Dearmer still apply, and certainly there is adequate provision for such processions in most Anglican collections of hymns. But sometimes a procession is made to a certain place like the crib or Easter garden, and prayers are said. The chopping up of a long hymn into two parts should happen only if the sense and structure of the hymn allow it; otherwise, two hymns are preferable.

There remains the question of what is called the 'office hymn'. This is a revival of the mediaeval practice whereby a hymn was sung in religious communities at the various offices of the day. It is doubtful whether they can be successfully transplanted into the offices of the BCP or ASB. Certainly, Thomas Cranmer drew from Vespers and Compline in his order of Evening Prayer. But he did create a new service; and whether by luck or genius, he placed the *Magnificat* between the Old and New Testament lessons. This forms a brilliant link, especially when we consider the position of the *Magnificat* in St. Luke's Gospel. But the splendid sequence is destroyed if a hymn is inserted after the first lesson in the interests of supposed antiquity. Percy Dearmer argued that the best place for an office hymn at Evengsong was before the psalms,[1] and although this would make the first part of the service rather cumbrous, it would have the advantage of setting the season quite early in the office and would be vastly preferable to the position often chosen for this hymn. Some recognition of this place for an office hymn is made in the ASB where the ancient *Phos Hilaron* may be sung before the psalms in the evening.

But, again, there are aesthetic objections to putting one kind of music directly after another — as in those churches which have the regrettable habit of singing a hymn immediately after the anthem. In the fairly rare instances in which the psalms are sung to plainsong, an office hymn in the same style of music would work very well. Another possibility for the plainsong office hymn might be, in some churches, in the place appointed for the anthem — perhaps especially if it were sung as such by a competent choir.

B. The Daily Office

So far we have considered Anglican Matins and Evensong as Sunday services, but, of course, they were originally designed as daily offices. The prominent part which they played in Anglican Sunday worship for four centuries is an accident of history. Their use on weekdays by only a very few of the laity seems to have been a fact throughout history. It is, moreover, curious that the same services should have been thought suitable for weekly use by a large congregation, and daily recitation by the clergy and a few others.

The different purposes of these services are given some recognition in the ASB. The longer forms of Morning and Evening Prayer which structurally resemble those of the Prayer Book are recommended for Sunday use. The shorter forms are derived from those originally devised by the Joint Liturgical Group. Both editions of the JLG's Daily Office[2] suggest the use of hymns as alternatives to canticles at Morning and Evening Prayer, and print lists of suggestions. But such lists are hardly exhaustive. The hymns could be seasonal, or related to the time of day at which they are sung, or they could arise from the passage(s) of scripture read in the service. Anglicans following their own rubrics could use hymns in addition to the canticles and probably at the end of the office. Some hymns are built into the more elaborate arrangements made for Morning and Evening Prayer in the Roman Catholic Church. Perhaps it would not be altogether impossible for small groups meeting to celebrate the office also to sing a hymn. Again, its devotional use by individuals could give richness and variety to the office: and to this use of hymnody we shall return in the last chapter.

C. Free Church Worship

We have seen that in the Free Churches, hymnody is an integral part of liturgy. Freedom in the way that the liturgy was compiled was claimed as part of the heritage of these traditions, and it is an heritage that many would still strongly defend.

Nevertheless, from the nineteenth century onwards, there has been an increase in the use of more set patterns of worship. Often they were considerably affected by the structure of Anglican Matins and Evensong. The Order of Morning Prayer in the 1936 Methodist Book of Office is closely akin to the Prayer Book. Though in theory setting a norm for Sunday worship, in fact its use was confined to a very small number of churches. The orders of morning and evening worship in the *Book of Common Order* 1940 show a similar relationship to the BCP in structure, though hardly at all in content.

A complete change may be noted in the current service-books of these two churches. The Methodist Service book 1975 has the Eucharist as 'The Sunday Service' and only secondarily offers an order of Sunday service without the Lord's Supper. The introduction runs:

> *In many churches of the Reformation tradition it has been the custom, once a Sunday, for the shape of the service to reflect that of the complete order of Word and Sacrament, even when there is no celebration of the Lord's Supper, and the outline that follows is offered as a guide for this purpose. Other outlines may be used for a second service.* [3]

The Book of Common Order (1979) has under 'The Divine Service' three full orders of Holy Communion and an 'outline order of service for public worship when the Lord's Supper is not celebrated'. Speaking of the experience of the Holy Spirit in the Presbyterian tradition of worship in Scotland, the introduction continues:

> *The Committee believes that the experience is richest where worship is ordered according to the eucharistic pattern, that is to say where the reading and preaching of the word lead to prayers of thanksgiving and intercession and all the fullness of eucharistic devotion save the partaking of bread and wine. This was the earlier tradition of the Reformed Church in Scotland and it is the order which the Committee believes best reflects the logic of the gospel.*[4]

In both these service-books, the Eucharist is regarded as the normative act of worship for Sundays; but despite the ideals and hopes of those who compiled them, there are few Methodist or Presbyterian churches in which the 'full' order of service including the Lord's Supper is held every Sunday. The reasons do not concern us here, but the result is that the structure of non-sacramental worship now tends to follow an 'ante-Communion' pattern rather than that of Matins or Evensong. As the Church of Scotland editors rightly claim, this is faithful to the pattern of worship envisaged by John Calvin and other reformers of the period.

For such services, many of the suggestions made in the last chapter will apply. They will certainly apply to opening hymns, and to those sung before or between readings. What has been said in this chapter about hymns before and after sermon in Anglican worship will have an echo for Free Church readers of this book. Methodism has generally seen the last hymn in the service as, in some sense, an act of dedication for the worshippers. In reformed churches a doxology is sometimes used at this point, though it is often subtly different from the act of praise with which the service might begin. Short hymns like Watts' *Come, dearest Lord, descend and dwell* (HP 725) or Conder's *Head of the church, our risen Lord* (HP 547) are often thought suitable to the close of worship, and point to the fulfilment of God's purpose, and the role which the Church is to play as His serving community.

But not all services are constructed in this way, and it is to be hoped that the creative use of hymnody which characterised Free Church worship at its best will continue to flourish there, and in other churches. For there are in most denominations occasions where special acts of worship need to be devised. We should not ignore the possibility of using hymns to express not only praise, but other forms of prayer. Not much of Wesley's 1780 classification remains in *Hymns and Psalms* but under 'the worshipping people' there are still sub-headings like 'confession and supplication' or 'petition and intercession' as indeed there are in many other hymn-books. Sometimes a hymn does not have to lead into or be supplemented by a prayer, for it is a prayer in itself. *Open, Lord my inward ear* (HP 540) might well say everything that needs to be said at the beginning of a retreat or Quiet Day, and *Behold, the servant of the Lord* (HP 788) might fulfil the same function at its close.

The phrase 'hymn-sandwich' is carelessly and often pejoratively bandied about by Anglicans when the service is different from their own norms of liturgy; and also by Free Churchmen who have had bitter experiences of acts of worship which seem to have no shape, and appear to be going in no particular direction. But, as I have remarked elsewhere, there is nothing wrong with a sandwich if it is properly made; an important ingredient is the hymn which can give flavour and interest to it.

D. Family Services

The Family Service often belongs to this style of worship which we have been discussing. In many Anglican and Free Churches, the Family Service occurs once a month, and in some it is even more frequent. There are Anglican parishes in which this is the only viable alternative to the Eucharist. In the Church of England, the phrase can mean a number of different things. It can simply mean the Eucharist at which the needs of children are given greater prominence than usual; or it can mean an adaptation or simplification of one of the liturgies in regular use; it can have a format which is almost invariably followed, or it can be specially devised on many, if not most occasions.

The popularity of family services in many churches is beyond doubt, but this sort of worship has its problems. Among them is the question of how to lead those who participate happily once a month into the more regular worship of the Church — and this raises the further question of how closely related to regular worship the family service should be. Again, if this is the principal (perhaps the only) service on a Sunday morning, it must surely also cater for those who are neither children themselves nor parents of young children. The word 'family' is meant to be inclusive, but it can seem exclusive to the single, the childless and to some whose marriages have broken.

The problems of the family service — pastoral, liturgical and theological — concern us here only in so far as they affect the hymnody selected for them.[5] And, since they vary so much in structure and in content, only a few general points are possible. First, there must be hymns and songs which appeal to and really involve the children present. This requires research and care as suggested in chapter 2; too often, children have been subjected to what their elders think they like or think they ought to like! Secondly, hymns and songs regularly used in the liturgy of the Church must be represented so that transitions to that liturgy can more easily be made. It is unfortunate when participants in family services become an isolated coterie, and worse still when children identify all worship with this form of it, and so put it away with all other childish things. The third point is that which has been made consistently in these pages; those who choose hymns, songs and choruses for family services must ask what they are for and what they are meant to do for the places in it at which they are chosen. When we think we want a hymn it is worth asking 'Why?' and that should lead us to ask what *kind* of hymn we really want.

The last question applies no less to those meetings and organisations which 'begin with a hymn'. Indeed 'begin with a hymn' is a phrase that needs a little examination. For often there will be prayers as well and perhaps a reading. Sometimes the hymn need not be absolutely at the beginning, but arise from or complement the prayers or reading used. A 'good' hymn depends for part of its goodness upon the time and place in which it is sung.

NOTES:

1. Dearmer, *The Parson's Handbook* (Humphrey Milford, 1931), p. 218.
2. R.C.D. Jasper (ed.), *The Daily Office* (SPCK and Epworth, 1968). *The Daily Office Revised* (SPCK, 1978).
3. *The Methodist Service Book* (Methodist Publishing House, 1975), p. B18.
4. *The Book of Common Order* (St Andrew's Press, 1979), p. viii.
5. There is a good discussion of them in Kenneth Stevenson *Family Services* (Alcuin Club/SPCK), 1981).

VI. HYMNS FOR SPECIAL SERVICES

The number of 'special services' held in all churches has increased considerably since the second world war, and continues to escalate. The weekly music sheets of Gloucester Cathedral indicate no kind of carol service at Christmas during the first thirty years of this century; at the present time, the building is used almost every night during the second part of Advent for organisations wanting this kind of service. In the Free Churches, many events which would once have been held on a week-night in the schoolroom now take place on Sunday in the church.

A. Carol Services

Probably no church of any tradition is without its carol service near Christmas. There are signs that, at last, the format devised in the last century for Truro Cathedral and popularised in this century by broadcasts from King's College, Cambridge, is no longer regarded as binding for these occasions. People are beginning to see that it is not necessary always to have *nine* lessons or a 'bidding' prayer, and some are even realising that there are alternatives to *Once in royal David's city* for the opening.

Where there is a choir, there is usually a division of labour between what is sung by the choir alone, and what is sung by the congregation as a whole. To achieve a balance between the two, and to ensure some connection between what is read in the lessons and what is sung in the carols and hymns is not easy. The main difficulty in the latter case is that nearly all Christmas music relates to one passage of scripture — Luke 2: 1-14. In some churches, what is assigned to the congregation is totally predictable and invariable. It is outside the scope of this book to say much about carols, but hymns for this occasion are our subject.

Many people do not make such a distinction. There is a tendency at Christmas to call everything sung by anybody a 'carol' so that the word is inappropriately applied to such items as *Hark! the herald angels sing* to Mendelssohn's tune. Here we make a plea for the inclusion of hymns that do not simply tell the story yet again (like *While Shepherds watched*) but for those which explore its meaning. *O little town of Bethlehem* is an example of such — especially if it can be wedded to Walford Davies' *Christmas Carol* which brings out the delicacy of its devotional quality. It is sad that so few of Wesley's great hymns on the Incarnation are known and used outside Methodism; *Let earth and heaven combine, Glory be to God on high* and *All glory to God in the sky* (HP 109, 101, 400) would offer an opportunity within our Christmas music for deeper meditation on the mystery of the Incarnation. Among modern contributors, the same could be said of Fred Pratt Green's *How dark was the night of his coming* (Anglican Praise 740).

Someone is bound to object that the music given to the congregation must be what they *know*. Here I offer two suggestions. First, the congregation need not be restricted to hymns; there are many carols in the strict sense of the word which people know and could sing. Secondly, there is a place at Christmas for a 'Songs of Praise' type service in which congregations could learn some fresh material as well as sing what they have come to regard as traditional. The next section of this chapter is devoted to this occasion of hymn-singing; suffice it to say here that since so many people enjoy singing Christmas music, this need not always be in the context of a formal service — certainly not one so stylised as the traditional carol service.

It is right that there should be an innocent and unsophisticated enjoyment of Christmas by Christians no less than anybody else. But in telling and re-telling the story, we should also seek to grow in our understanding both of its eternal message and in its particular relevance to our own time. Surely this can be conveyed through texts and music that do not have to be ponderous or didactic in consequence. But there is one area for which hymn-writing is specially needed, and that is for the *end* of the Christmas Eucharist or for the conclusion of other acts of worship at this season. There is very little that 'sends us out' with new vision and resolution.

There are many other occasions in the year when the format of the carol service — that is, a sequence of readings with music by choir and congregation — might be used. Advent carol services have become increasingly popular in recent years.[1] Despite the problems caused by the weather, a service of this character at Epiphany-tide could cheer the January days, and help lift congregations from the doldrums into which they easily fall after Christmas. If all three carol services are held, they could be linked; Advent could concentrate on the Old Testament preparation for Christ's coming, Christmas on the story itself and Epiphany on the significance of the Incarnation as set out in other parts of the New Testament. In some churches, this could be illustrated by the movement of the choir, and in some the use of non-biblical readings could be a commentary on the scriptures themselves. There is room, too, for this sort of service during Lent and at

Easter, at Pentecost, All Saints-tide and Harvest to name but a few. The Royal School of Church Music has provided a number of services of this sort, and these can generally be adapted for use by churches with very limited musical resources.

In *Interpreting Worship* I suggested the use of this style of service for presenting the message of one book (or section of a book) in the Bible, and an appendix offers, as an example, such a sequence for Jonah*. Because of the nature of this present book, the discussion is restricted to hymns, and in many churches, this may be the only possibility. But there is a place here for choir or instrumentalists, for mime or for dance — and obviously at certain points for spoken prayers which complement rather than re-state what has been read or sung. In most acts of worship, we are, of necessity, restricted to fairly short excerpts from scripture, and the more detailed and connected study of books is left to bible-study groups. But in days when knowledge of the scriptures is often minimal, there is a case for getting to grips with some part of them during Sunday worship. In some places, Sunday evening services would be ideal for this purpose. In others, this would be suitable, with obvious adaptations, for the family services discussed in the last chapter.

B. 'Songs of Praise' Services

The title of this popular television programme — itself taken from that of a famous hymn-book — is now repeated in a good many churches. This sort of service is used at anniversaries and missions, the conclusion of flower festivals and many other occasions.

It is full of oportunities for the use of hymnody. First, it provides for maximum participation by the congregation who may well be involved in the choice of the hymns as well as in the singing of them. Secondly, it allows an opportunity for introducing new material. If people have sung several hymns which they know and like, they are more ready to learn something new than when it is sprung upon them in the course of normal liturgy; and the relaxed atmosphere is itself a better setting for learning and trying out new tunes. Thirdly, it permits the commentator to say something about the hymns and tunes that are sung. People seem to be interested in the history of hymns — especially if there is a story behind them — and are consequently receptive of the message contained in them. Fourthly, here is a chance for some one to make

*See appendix on page 88

all sorts of points which will help to improve the standard of singing. Congregations can be encouraged to stand up as soon as the hymn is played over, to be ready to sing when the hymn starts; to take breaths at suitable times and not always at the end of the lines; to sing both softly and loudly; and, in general, so to sing that they bring out the sense of the hymn.

The spin-off for regular worship is obvious. The congregation is likely, as a result, to pay more attention to the hymns themselves, and to the good singing of them. What is learned in 'Songs of Praise' can have a beneficial effect on the whole of worship. But the occasion is worth-while in itself — though once again it requires care and trouble in its planning. It could be no more than a sentimental and rather indolent occasion.

There is a variety of ways in which the service can be planned. As in the BBC TV programme, people can be invited to make a choice, and then to tell the others why the hymn means something to them. This can be a very moving form of witness — provided that those who make these contributions can speak with reasonable brevity and coherence, and above all, *audibly*. Alternatively, people can be invited to make a choice, and to submit this to the minister or whoever is appointed to comment on the hymns. They can then be arranged in some sort of sequence, though the commentators who link them will certainly need tact in speaking of hymns that they personally dislike! It need hardly be said that all choices should be made well in advance of the service itself. A Vicar once decided on impulse not to preach on a particular Sunday, but instead to do an impromptu 'Songs of Praise' by inviting the congregation at sermon time to choose favourite hymns which were then sung. This meant that no one had a chance to think about the matter; the Vicar could not make any considered comment, and the organist had no chance to work out the proper accompaniment of the various verses. It may be worth saying at this point that whereas any competent musician can play a hymn-tune, the accompaniment of a hymn that helps the congregation to do its best and which brings out the meaning of what is sung is a skill that needs practice. Sometimes it is one which a very gifted organist has not fully acquired. Finally, it is important that a service of this kind should not be too long. It can very easily over-run its time; and if too many requests are received, it is better to reserve some for a future occasion than to allow legs, voices and minds to be weary of the whole process. Once upon a time, children were told to leave the table 'feeling that they would like a little more'.

It is good when congregations leave the church in the same mood.

But 'Songs of Praise' can have a more specialised theme. We have already mentioned its use at Christmas. Again, this allows the congregation to have a more extended 'sing' than is possible even at a carol service, and it also allows many things to be said about the carols and hymns themselves. Some texts — especially those from the Middle Ages — need explanation, and *Here we bring new water* is an example. There is also the chance to bring out the theology and wealth of biblical allusion in a hymn like Charles Wesley's *Let earth and heaven combine* and to ask what *It came upon the midnight clear* was meant to do when it written, and what it can do now — preferably in the revised version of H & P 108. There are thus endless opportunities of exploring the history and theology of what we sing, and of helping the carols and hymns to be true aids to worship today. Organists and musical directors can be no less involved as they help people to sing hymns and carols in such a way as to comprehend their meaning and significance. I believe that such an occasion is not just instructive to congregations and helpful to their devotions, but that it can contribute to the sheer *enjoyment* of what they sing. People soon find that it is more fun to sing well than to sing badly.

What applies to Christmas applies no less to other seasons not so well endowed with hymns and carols. At Easter, comment can be made on the variety of ways in which writers have interpreted the resurrection of Christ, and perhaps on the liturgical occasions for which such hymns were written. We can notice how some hymns tell the story, others comment on its significance, and most do both. The use of Old Testament imagery in many of the Easter hymns can be explored. And here is an opportunity to introduce contributions by contemporary writers who offer hymns for this festival because there is something that they believe needs saying: two fine examples are Brian Wren's *Christ is alive* (H & P 190) and Christopher Idle's *If Christ had not been raised again* (Anglican Praise 746).

These criteria can be applied to 'Songs of Praise' arranged for Ascensiontide, Pentecost, and other occasions in the year. Perhaps on some 'ordinary' Sunday, such a service might be arranged on the theme of the day, and people be asked to suggest not just their favourite hymn, but their favourite hymn on a particular subject. The 7th Sunday before Easter (ASB) or the 20th after Pentecost appear as possibilities for this. Mention was made earlier of the monotonous effect of a choice of hymns that simply spells out the theme in almost every verse; but here the choices of different people might contribute to that allusiveness that was recommended in our treatment of this matter.

If 'Songs of Praise' is a regular feature in the life of a church (i.e. if it is held perhaps quarterly) there are still further possibilities. One of these would be an exploration of the work of a particular writer. The celebration in 1988 of the 250th anniversary of the conversions of John and Charles Wesley meant that up and down the country festivals celebrated their massive contribution to hymnody. In such, the problem was not what to choose but what to leave out. It would be more difficult with a writer like George Herbert — usually represented in our books by no more than half a dozen items, none of which was originally intended to be a hymn. None the less, in this instance, the service could focus on his life and ministry, and could well include readings from his poetry and prose.

It is less easy to do this in the case of composers. The tunes derived from Orlando Gibbons would, for all their excellence, be somewhat monotonous if they provided the sole musical diet for the occasion. The prolific contributions made by the nineteenth century composers S.S. Wesley and J.B. Dykes might just be possible. It would be good to do the same thing for the twentieth-century composer, Cyril Taylor, if only to show that *Abbot's Leigh* is not his only fine hymn-tune; but for most people, this would be almost entirely a learning occasion, and not at all what they expected by 'Songs of Praise'. Perhaps the best method would be to take a number of composers of a certain period of history, and the same might be done for those hymn-writers who have made a minor but distinguished contribution to the hymnody of the Church.

C. Annual and One-off Celebrations

We move to an area in which there is far less room for manoevure — to those annual services which have the needs of an organisation in mind. In all churches this will include Remembrance Sunday which, it should be remembered, is not quite the property of the British Legion, despite the excellent work done by them on Poppy Day, and the help which they give in other ways to those suffering as a result of conflict. In large city centre churches, there may well be a civic service, and, according to area and church, there will be a number of organisations for which an annual service has to be arranged.

Often the representatives of such organisations have a stereotyped and rather rigid idea of the structure of the service. There are at least two reasons for this. One is that the service itself has become traditional, and the organisers of it see themselves as guardians of a tradition. The other is that the annual service of an organisation is in some cases the annual service of many who attend it, and they have little idea of how the Church has moved on in its thinking and its liturgy. Consequently, there is an almost invariable request for hymns that 'everybody knows'.

As we have seen, this is a request that is very difficult to meet — despite the good intentions of those who seek to do so. Some people attending these services know hardly any hymns at all. What was known by an earlier generation is not always known by this one. Some hymns that were still popular in the middle of this century have gone out of fashion — *Nearer, my God to thee* and *For ever with the Lord,* for example. It is interesting to compare the present authorised forms of service for Remembrance Sunday with their immediate pre-decessors; some of the hymns which now appear for the first time are a reflection of present-day use and taste. It is even more instructive to see, where records are accessible, what was sung for this occasion in the 'fifties or the 'thirties. The variety in age and experience of those attending such a service makes it difficult to get it right for everybody.

For these occasions, it is useful to compile lists of hymns suited to different points in the service. These will include hymns of adoration for the beginning and hymns of dedication for the close. A fairly permanent structure will suggest the other kinds of hymns that are required. A list of hymns of praise may not throw up any surprises, yet as it is prepared, it may include some that have not been thought of before, and it will at least ensure some variety from year to year. It is also good to have some hymns — or at least their tunes — on tape to play to representatives of organisations who come to arrange a service. People do not always recognise a hymn from its first line; *Ye that know the Lord is gracious* may seem unknown, but *Hyfrydol* is not. Organisations should be discouraged from regarding too many items as those which they 'always have'. There is a need for continuity, but also a need for constant, if slight amendment. One organisation, only just ten years old, has already acquired two hymns which it regards as unchangeable; since there are usually five in this service, the situation is not catastrophic, but if this sort of thing grows, it discourages creative thought from the membership, which must obviously change with the years.

Many annual services are, of course, arranged for organisations of younger people such as Scouts and Guides. Here it is worth repeating what was said in the last chapter about family services. There must be a real attempt to find out hymns that have meaning for the young people concerned rather than the assumption that their elders know what they want to sing! This is always changing — and can sometimes change quite rapidly.

Finally we turn to those services which are not annual, but 'one-off'. In 1988, the WRVS celebrated its golden jubilee, and services were held in various centres. Where a school has to close down, there may be a request for a special service to mark the occasion. There may be the dedication of a new building or emblem, or the inauguration of some new kind of work. In all circumstances for which a special service is projected, it is best to start by discussing with the members of the organisation what it is they are really celebrating and what it is that they want to say in their act of worship. After such discussions, it is possible to get some structure for the service, and only to begin choosing the hymns when this has been done. By this means, we are more likely to arrive at what is appropriate for the occasion, and less dependent upon what happen to be the favourites of two or three members of the committee.

The nature of some organisations means that sometimes there must be new hymnody[2] — since there is nothing in the conventional repertoire that adequately reflects what they are trying to do. A case in point is an organisation concerned with conservation of the natural order; *All things bright and beautiful* may have a place in such a service, but we need to move on to something less naive and less general — such as *Lord bring the day to pass* (H&P 347). The same has been found to be true for the various peace movements that ask for church services. Sometimes it is possible to set new words to familiar tunes; but this is not always so, and sometimes again, although a tune may technically 'fit' the words, the text somehow cries out for its own music. When this is the case there are two possibilities: (a) the organisation might be asked to practise the hymn at its meetings, or (b) there might be a rehearsal for it before the service begins. Occasional churchgoers often arrive much earlier than those who regularly attend, and the time could usefully be spent in singing the less familiar hymns.

On the whole, those whose main concern is with the future are more ready to learn new things than those whose main concern is with the past. This is hardly surprising; but why is concern for the future so rare?

NOTES

1. There are useful suggestions for them in Michael Perham, *Liturgy Pastoral and Parochial* (SPCK, 1984).
2. Reginald Heber was commissioned by his father-in-law to write a missionary hymn for use the following day, and 'From Greenland's icy mountains' was the result. This is an example not generally to be imitated, but there are people capable of writing a hymn to order if given a reasonable amount of time and the fullest information about the cause and event. This could be a point of interest in such services.

VII. HYMNS FOR PARTICULAR RITES

A. Christian Initiation

Older clergy were brought up with the phrase 'occasional offices' to describe the services of baptism, marriage and burial. The sociological emphasis of the 1960s saw the expression 'rites of passage' often used for the same occasions. Both phrases assume that all three are of the same character, and may be regarded chiefly as personal and family occasions. By treating baptism in the same chapter as weddings and funerals, I do not intend to re-inforce this assumption.

(1) Baptism

Many Anglicans have long been campaigning for the restoration of baptism to the normal liturgy on Sundays. 'Restoration' is indeed the correct word since the first rubrics of the BCP Ministration of Public Baptism of Infants not only commend the practice but add two excellent reasons why it should be so. The ASB says that the baptism of children should normally be at Holy Communion or at Morning or Evening Prayer, and, using the reasons given in the Prayer Book, recommends that 'at other times, regular members of the congregation should attend the service'. Moreover, the ASB rubrics show how both the order of Holy Communion and that of baptism can be shortened when the two are combined — thereby ensuring that the whole act of worship is not over-long in consequence.

When celebrated during the Eucharist, the baptismal liturgy follows the ministry of the word. The same practice is followed in the Church of Scotland and the United Reformed Church. Methodists do not specify the point in liturgy, but say that baptism 'is normally administered at a main service of public worship'. In these last three churches, this is far less of a novelty than it seems in some Anglican parishes. Needless to say, in the Baptist and other churches where baptism is restricted to believers, the occasion has always been one of great solemnity and significance for the local worshipping community. The conference of Faith and Order at Lima recognised that both traditions of baptism were likely to continue; but with ecumenical sensitivity recommended the avoidance of any kind of casualness to those churches in which infant baptism is normal.

When baptism is administered publicly in this way, there are three possible places for hymnody. A hymn may be sung between the ministry of the word and the baptism, and the Book of Common Order recommends that infants are brought into the church during the singing of it. A hymn may be sung during the baptism service itself. This is suggested in the ASB where the hymn is inserted between the 'decision' and the actual baptism, and in some churches this will accompany a procession to the font. When the baptism has taken place, the ASB recommends that the Eucharist should be resumed at the Peace, and the next hymn will be in its normal place in that liturgy. In other churches baptism may or may not be followed by Holy Communion; if it is not, the service will probably end at this point with a concluding hymn.

It is unlikely that hymns will be sung at all three places suggested, but where they are (a) the first hymn will be one of preparation for what is to take place and may include invocation of the Holy Spirit (b) the second hymn will be directly related to the baptism itself and (c) the third hymn could refer to the homes of the children and to family life. If (b) is not used, the final hymn may be 'baptismal' in character and if (c) is sung at the Eucharist, it is more likely to refer to what is to follow rather than to what has just taken place.

Until recently, there has been a dearth of good hymns on baptism. Often they have focussed on what is secondary rather than on what is primary. Among Methodists, *See Israel's gentle Shepherd stand* was much favoured with its reference to Jesus' willingness to receive children. Anglicans often chose *In token that thou shalt not fear* which refers to the signing with the cross. *By cool Siloam's shady rill* was once regarded as *the* baptismal hymn in the Kirk — until its partial banishment from the third edition of the *Church Hymnary*. It has now been restored in the supplement to that book *(Songs of God's People)*, and is basically a hymn about spiritual education. None of these hymns, it must be noted, refers to the central action of the service — namely the pouring of water in the name of the Trinity. Moreover, there has been a general and understandable assumption that baptism is always for *infants*. Interestingly, the old standard edition of *Hymns Ancient and Modern* included a Wesley hymn written specifically for the baptism of adults which was omitted in the 1950 revision. I have tried to avoid value-judgements on hymn-books, but feel bound to say that I believe *Hymns and Praise* to have the best collection of hymns for this sacrament to be found in any contemporary book. There are hymns suitable for adults and children as well as infants, and there hymns which speak of the central significance of the sacrament rather than its secondary implications.

But adult baptism, which once seemed so rare, has, for a variety of reasons, become more common in recent years, and is likely to increase. All the service-books which we have quoted provide for it, and in the ASB, the full order of Baptism, Confirmation and Holy Communion is the norm from which others are derived. In the *Methodist Service Book* of 1975, both this order and that of Confirmation and Holy Communion have hymns actually printed in the text of the service, although the rubric states that others may be used. For adult baptism, this book recalled *Come Father, Son and Holy Ghost* banished from the 1933 book, but restored to *Hymns and Psalms*. AMNS has one hymn (506) which is suitable for candidates who are not infants.

(2) Confirmation

For confirmation, it has long been customary to choose hymns from all over the books, and again, AMNS has only one hymn specifically designated. Many Anglican bishops would welcome the widest possible selection for these services which they conduct for a large part of the year; some have found it necessary to issue directives about the kind of hymnody required at different points in the service, and others have reported such solecisms as the choosing of hymns invoking the Holy Spirit *after* the confirmation has taken place. At such services, the opening hymn will be seasonal or an act of praise; hymns between readings will refer to the theme of the passages chosen; the hymn after the sermon (or perhaps the renewal of baptismal vows) could be one of invocation, and if there is no celebration of Holy Communion, the last hymn one of dedication. But it is increasingly common in the Church of England to celebrate confirmation within the Eucharist, and this seems to be almost invariable in other churches we have mentioned. Episcopal confirmation means that in many Anglican parishes, the rite may be administered at a festival, and the proper lessons of that festival read. The rubrics of the ASB makes clear that on other occasions, the bishop may direct readings that are not included in the wide selection provided for the service. All this extends the range of hymnody that is possible. The debate continues in the Church of England as to whether confirmation should still be regarded as the form of admission to communion;

if the eventual answer were negative, it might have new implications not only for hymnody, but for liturgy itself.

B. Weddings

It is now unusual for hymns at a wedding to have a direct connection with the occasion. Hymns were once chosen from a very small canon — perhaps because of the social conditions of the time, and perhaps because they were the only ones offered by more authoritarian clergy. The only survivor from the wedding hymns found in our books in the earlier part of this century is *O perfect love* still often set to the Barnby tune which, curiously, never appeared in the various editions of *Hymns Ancient and Modern*. Many of our contemporary writers have turned their attention to hymns for the marriage service, feeling that this is a gap which needs to be filled. AMNS has contributions from Ian Fraser and Basil Bridge, and in H&P the latter is joined by Brian Wren and Fred Pratt Green. All four hymns are set to tunes that are not unfamiliar. How far they will 'catch on' remains to be seen. In 1950, the revisers of A&M included two wedding hymns to very well-known tunes, but both have disappeared from the new standard edition — presumably, because of lack of demand. The efforts of our contemporary writers certainly deserve a better fate; for they have asked fresh questions about marriage, and have tried to write verse that is sensitive without being too sentimental.

The recoil from 'wedding' hymns has come about for two probable reasons. First, there is once again, the understandable insistence that the hymns must be *known*. I have mentioned that the tunes for the newer hymns are not unfamiliar, and at least one of them is very well-known. But it seems that many people do not want to be confronted with a new text on such occasions.

Secondly, the choice of hymns has sometimes been seen as a way in which the service can be distinctive for those who are being married; much of the service is provided for them, but here is a chance for them to make their own contribution to it.

Fortunately, it is no longer the only way. The ASB has an important rubric which runs:

> *Instead of the additional prayers (section 31-38) prayers which the couple have written or selected in co-operation with the priest may be used.*

And in conformity with its usual practice, this book offers a wide selection of readings that are appropriate. The other books which we have considered do not make such flexibility explicit, but it does nevertheless belong to the traditions which they represent.

People being married today have therefore a considerable part to play in the designing of the service. The minister who prepares them will no longer say 'This is the service; now what hymns would you like?' Instead, he will discuss the various options with them, and when the form has been decided go on to suggest places in it where there might be hymns, psalms or other musical contributions. This could go some way to avoiding those bizarre choices which have been the subject of jokes too hoary to be repeated here. 'It's always been my favourite hymn' may still be said of *Jerusalem* and it must be taken seriously, yet met with the question 'Where do you think it would fit in this service?' The time and trouble taken over the preparation of the service will almost invariably be appreciated, and not least by those who have little contact with the Church. And it may well be a means whereby there is an increase of understanding not only of marriage, but of God whose gift it is.

Marriage within the context of the Eucharist has long been the norm in the Roman Catholic Church, and is growing, with varying degrees of speed in other churches. The ASB suggests two ways in which this can be structured. In the first of these, there could be a hymn near the beginning of the service, or between readings, another after the sermon and before the marriage itself, a third after the Peace and the final one before the blessing. If four hymns seemed too heavy for the occasion, any one or more of these could be omitted.

In a marriage service without communion, there are three places for hymns; the first is again near the beginning of the service or between readings if there is more than one; after the marriage itself and before the prayers (and readings/address if used at this point) and before the final blessing. Again, many people want only two hymns, and any one of the three can be omitted. The new hymns on marriage which we have mentioned are suitable to all three points, especially perhaps the second and third. Other sorts of hymnody include (a) near the beginning an act of praise or thanksgiving for all God's gifts, especially that of love and (b) at the close a hymn which expresses the dedication to Him of this new way of life. Hymns about Christian love have seemed appropriate and in H&P, Charles Wesley's *Thou God of truth and love* has found its way into this section. A small, but worthwhile consideration, is that hymns after the marriage should, if possible, be in the plural rather than the singular; 'I' and 'me' can, of course be understood in a corporate sense, but, psychologically it seems better at this stage to sing of 'we' and 'us'.[1]

There are other moments in the service where hymns might be used, but it is important that they should help the service flow rather than impede its progress. A few years ago, there was a fashion in some Anglican churches to sing a hymn at the entrance of the bride; this seemed to do justice neither to the hymn nor to the entrance of the bride!

The Book of Common Order 1979 prints a list of hymns that are suitable for the occasion and taken from the official hymn-book of the Kirk. In *These Are The Hymns*, I offered two short lists of hymns suitable to the beginning and end of the service. This I now hesitate to do for reasons implied or stated in this book. But I am sure that it is desirable for those who regularly officiate at weddings to compile their own lists, and to have some hymns on tape — since so often it is the tune that determines their choice.

C. Funerals
(1) Funeral services

'Funeral' hymns have become as rare as those for weddings — and for the same two reasons as those mentioned in the last section. But in the case of funerals, we must add a third. This has to do with the evasion of the fact of death which has been noted in so much writing on this subject. It is often expressed in such phrases as 'we don't want anything mournful'. This kind of comment could be the result of a faith in the resurrection so strong that natural sorrow seemed almost out of place; it could arise from a real anxiety about 'getting through' the service; but it could also mean that those attending a funeral want to think as little as possible about death.

So John Ellerton's beautiful *Now the labourer's task is o'er* and Wesley's robust *Rejoice for a brother deceased* have not only gone out of fashion, but disappeared from contemporary collections altogether.

Instead we find a resurgence of *The Old Rugged Cross* for reasons which baffle the present writer as *Crimond* and *Abide with me* did not. Far more general hymns like *Praise my soul* or *The day thou gavest* are frequently chosen — again, perhaps because they are sure to be known, or were favourites of the deceased or the mourners.

On this subject, contemporary hymn-writers have been far less prolific. Even the table of contents in hymn-books seems to shy away from the subject. If we look again at the two hymn-books to which most constant reference has been made, we find that whereas the 1933 *Methodist Hymn Book* had a section entitled 'death, judgement, future life' and another for 'funerals and memorial services', there are no corresponding sections in *Hymns and Psalms*. One hymn for a funeral, written by Fred Kaan appears under 'occasional services' and the book concludes with 'The Church Triumphant' in which relatively small section we must look for hymns like *Come let us join our friends above*. The New Standard Version of *Hymns Ancient and Modern* has in its table of contents only one hymn under 'funerals and commemorations', and there are none listed in the subject-index to the supplements; but suggestions are offered under 'Additional hymns for various times and church seasons'.

At a Christian funeral, there is a place for grief as well as a place for hope. An expositor of the burial service in the Prayer Book once said that you could not hear the message of 1 Corinthians 15 until you had heard that of Psalm 90. There is a place for much else besides thanksgiving for the life of someone much loved, and prayer, in the words of the ASB that we may have 'the wisdom and the grace to use aright the time that life left to us here on earth'. Not all these emotions and prayers can be expressed in the hymns that are chosen, but they should certainly have some bearing upon the choice.

We turn again to the service-books, and the positions which they suggest for hymnody. The ASB suggests one after the readings (and sermon) and one before the final commendation. The Methodists suggest one near the beginning and one at the end of the service. Similar provision is made in other orders, and it is implied or stated that hymns and psalms may be used before readings if more than one should be chosen. As in the case of weddings, the *Book of Common Order* has a suggested list of hymns.

It is again useful for clergy and ministers to have such a list, and wherever possible to discuss the matter with the family rather than be presented with the choice by the undertaker. Modern conditions mean that there is often a long gap between death and cremation, and when the funeral arrangements are made, it is not necessary to reach *immediate* conclusions about the content of the service unless it is to be specially printed. This can prevent decisions made by a wild guess, or a frantic search through the hymn-book, and can allow the family a couple of days to discuss possibilities among themselves.

Guidelines worth using are:

1. Hymns about the communion of saints — our relationship with those who have gone before us. *Ye holy angels bright* marvellously combines cheerfulness with relevance to the occasion. Baxter's other moving hymn *He wants not friends that hath thy love* could well be considered; a tune must be found for it, since it lacks a convincing and obvious musical partner. *For all the saints* would seem to many of us to be claiming a bit too much — even when the word 'saint' is used in its strict New Testament sense.
2. Hymns about the resurrection, readily located in the Easter sections and their cross-references in our hymn books, and including *Jesus lives, Thine be the glory* and *Now is eternal life*.
3. Hymns of trust and faith, widely scattered over most of our hymn-books.

Some people will already have a clear idea of what they want, and others may be acting on instructions in the dead person's will. If it is included in the latter, it can save much agonising in families. Again, the use of a piano or tape is to be recommended, as people have different ideas about what is the 'right' tune — for such hymns as *Jesu, lover of my soul* or *The King of love my shepherd is,* and most of all (if it should be chosen) *O Jesus, I have promised.* There comes the question of the odd, or even embarrassing choice directed by the deceased or requested by the mourners. No one wants to deny Grandpa his favourite hymn at his own funeral, and in such cases reference might be made in an address to the reason for its choice, and its apparent incongruity thus explained.

(2) Thanksgiving services

The above title seems now to be more commonly used than 'memorial service'. It was the kind of occasion once restricted to the prominent and the illustrious, but there are circumstances in which a family finds it desirable to have a private funeral, and then later a service of thanksgiving at a time possible for those who have to travel a considerable distance.

For such occasions, our service-books make no provision. The report of the Anglican Liturgical Commission which influenced the present shape of the funeral service did say that some parts of it might be suitable for a memorial service. This may indeed be right for occasions when this is considered the public form of the funeral. But more often, it is not a replica of that service which is required; it is, as its title suggests, a time in which to give thanks for the life of a particular person.

As I have just said, there is no set form or order to be followed here. A tested and possible structure could be (a) an act of thanksgiving for the life and gifts of the deceased with (where desired) the commendation of his or her soul to God (b) a 'ministry of the word' which would include, but not be restricted to passages from the Bible, and which would probably involve an address and (c) an act of intercession in which the congregation could remember the interests and activities of the person concerned, and pray that they might be continued by the living. The freedom of the occasion can be reflected in the freedom of the choice of hymns.

This chapter has dealt, in the main, with personal occasions for which some element of personal choice might be expected. In such cases 'favourite' hymns are likely to be advanced, and sometimes, as we have seen, their suitability to the occasion may be in question. The next chapter will be concerned with hymns as a means of growth and nurture, and perhaps it will encourage the idea of more than one favourite hymn; people who understand hymns and care about them are likely to have favourite hymns for the different seasons, favourite hymns of praise, favourite hymns of trust and so forth. By this means people who choose hymns for sensitive and personal occasions may be led to ask not just 'What do I like?', but 'What do I want to say (sing about) at *this* time?'

NOTES

1. The RSCM booklet *The Marriage Service with music* (1982), has 23 hymns, under the headings Praise, Marriage, Dedication.

VIII. HYMNS AS A MEANS OF GROWTH AND NURTURE

In one of his novels, Howard Spring takes us back to the end of the last century, to a humble street in Manchester and to the home of a Methodist local preacher. On Saturday evening, his wife would lay out on the kitchen table the things he would need in preparation for the next day: pens, ink, writing paper, blotting paper, the Bible, the concordance — and the hymn book. This last would be needed for more than the choosing of hymns; for it would influence the thought of the preacher, and the content of his sermon.

Perhaps no part of the Christian Church has so much valued hymns as the Methodist — because, as we have seen, they have so much influenced the liturgy, doctrine and devotion of its members. The Methodist emphasis on hymnody is arguably its greatest contribution to the whole Church, and one from which we can all learn. But Methodists are not the only people who love hymns.

Hymns are a means of growth and nurture for all. They can deepen and enlarge our understanding and our practice of the Christian Faith. This is likely to happen only if we possess at least one hymn-book — probably the one in use at the church which we attend. We must be able to look up hymns if we really want to use them.

A. Hymns in church

The use of hymns at home depends to a large extent on the way that they are used in church. It is only when hymns seem to matter there that people will find that they matter elsewhere. This book has been concerned with the choice of hymns at the various occasions at which a congregation meets. It has emphasised the care which this choice demands, and its aim has been that, through this care, people should sing the right hymn at the right time.

There are one or two other things that need to be said about the use of hymns in church. The first concerns their *announcement*. It is faintly chilling when the first words of worship are 'Hymn five hundred and eighty-four: five-eight-four', and not much better when this sort of formula is used in the course of it. The exercise takes on more meaning when the leader of worship says 'Let us sing a hymn of praise to God' or 'We take up the thought of this passage as we sing ...'. Such introductions do not have to be verbose, and they can very quickly become hackneyed. But there is a case — at least on occasions — for telling the congregation why they are about to sing a particular hymn. There may even be times when it is desirable to say something about the history or theology of the hymn. As a previous chapter suggested, this is best done, especially in extended format, at a service like 'Songs of Praise', but brief introductions are, from time to time, possible at regular services.

In some churches, of course, the hymns are not announced at all. People rely on the hymn-boards for information about what they are to sing. This may not be easy for everyone, and we tend to make more provision for the hard of hearing than for the short of sight. More frequently, there is a notice-sheet with the numbers of the hymns printed on it. One such contained a note that 'starred verses are always omitted'. This practice has two disadvantages; first it is easily overlooked by newcomers and strangers, and secondly it places too much reliance on the wisdom of those who edit our hymn-books. There are many occasions on which it is desirable to shorten a hymn or to sing only a part of it. But the way in which it is shortened may vary. I have mentioned the varied occasions on which *Hail to the Lord's anointed* might be sung. In AMNS verses 2 and 4 are asterisked. That might be the right selection for Epiphany with which the hymn is frequently associated. But on another occasion — such as following the ASB introductory sentence on the 8th Sunday before Easter — verse 2 would certainly be needed, and verse 5 might not. When hymn-numbers are printed on a service-sheet, there must be clear and underlined directions about which verses are to be sung by whom. If a verse is designated for trebles only, that should be mentioned — nothing is so justifiably irritating to congregations than doubt about whether or not they are supposed to sing. If a different tune is chosen, that should be noted; some people do bring tune-books, and, ideally, all should have a melody edition. And the notice-sheets could similarly provide such brief notes about hymns as would be made if they were announced.

Something usually needs to be said about hymns and tunes that are new to the congregation. Again, a service like 'Songs of Praise' provides an ideal setting for their introduction. But this service is probably not held very frequently, and many of those present on Sunday morning were not there at the last 'Songs of Praise'. Aids to learning new tunes include: (a) the use by the congregation of a hymn book that has the treble line of music (b) the playing over of the whole tune — perhaps twice (c) the singing of a verse or two by the choir in unison or by solo voice. Churches which do not have choirs might well have someone in the congregation who could do this (d) when such resources are not available, the use of a tape. It is often possible to use five minutes before the service for the learning of a hymn; but when everyone arrives at the last minute, it must be done in the course of the service itself. This is not the only matter about worship that requires the close and *advance* co-operation between those who have some part in leading it — president, preacher, organist and leader of intercessions. We must try to avoid the complaint that the service was too long.

Techniques for introducing new hymns are important, but attitudes matter even more. If our God is seen as the One who goes before us and as the One who is always doing new things for His people, then there should be willingness on their part to try new things and to welcome new forms of praise. Resistance to any kind of change can be the result of a static view of God and a neglect of the third person of the Trinity. Of course people need stablility as well as change; but acceptance of this principle does not deny its converse. Attitudes to hymns are, therefore, in any congregation, closely related to what it believes about God, and how it understands its own mission in the world.

But people meeting on Sundays are at various levels of understanding, and come with a variety of needs. New material must therefore be introduced gradually and sensitively. It must not be presented in a dictatorial manner, but equally it must not be the occasion of an apology. Instead, it must be seen as a joyful and exciting event. When people see why hymns matter, they will sing them better and use them more effectively.

B. Hymns at home

We turn from the public to the private use of hymns. The worship of the community as a whole affects the way in which the members worship by themselves.

So, in the first place, members of our congregations can be encouraged to make further use of what they have already experienced in church. The value of the Sunday service will be increased for them if they read again the lessons which have been heard in church, make simple notes on the sermon for continued meditation, use the material on the notice sheets as part of their own prayer. To all this we add the hymns — assuming by this stage that they have been carefully chosen, and closely related to the act of worship in which they were sung.

The hymn-book can be further used to assist whatever scheme of private devotion is used by members of the congregation. Reference has already been made to the daily office, and the possible use of hymnody in the course of it. But if less formal ways of prayer are preferred, hymnody can still be part of them. Hymns can express adoration, confession, thanksgiving and supplication (the famous ACTS), or ways of prayer that have other titles, and the index, or table of contents in the hymn-book will show where they are to be found. Most people need something with which to focus their thoughts; the hymn is only one possibility, but it is a strong one. Similarly, the hymn-book can supplement bible-study. We have noted that some hymn-books have a scriptural index to their contents. After reading and pondering a passage from the Bible and reading some comment upon it', the index would show us how it has been expressed or used by hymn writers. And this could be a means whereby study led to prayer and dedication.

The hymn-book can also be used in a more spontaneous way. In many hotels, Bibles are provided by the Gideons, and within their covers are suggestions about what to read in various circumstances or difficulties. A hymn-book with a good index can fulfil a similar role.

For all such uses, we need hymn books that have the fullest possible index to their contents, although we can make our own notes within. An earlier chapter has said something about the way in which hymn-books are set out. And even better use can be made of them with a commentary on their contents.

C. Hymns ready for replacement

Great claims have been made in this book for the potential influence of hymns. It has concentrated on the subject of what is appropriate, but there has been little reference to what is intrinsically good or bad in hymns. The first chapter stressed that they should be doctrinally acceptable and true in what they say about Christian experience; but the same chapter claimed a place for those which are allusive to doctrine rather than statements of it, and for those which point to experiences which are not yet ours but to which we hope to attain. Reference was later made to those songs which say the same thing over and over again in a very simple way, and these were seen as an ingredient but not the sole diet of the rations that we need for our journey. But apart from all these considerations, there are surely hymns which are bad in themselves as well as those which are good.[1]

There are few hymns of which I want to be totally dismissive, although there are many which I would be glad not to have to sing again. I would not want to rule out anything which has been genuinely helpful to Christian people at some stage in their pilgrimage. But no hymn book can contain everything that might have served such a purpose, and the selectivity involved in the making of a book can be agonising for its editors.

My axe would fall first of all on all hymns that are trite and dull, those which contain no lines that are memorable (in a good sense) and too many that are weak and feeble. Some second or third rate hymns need to be retained until something better is written on the same subject. One very barren area in this respect is that of ordination. It is a subject that has inspired little new hymnody — perhaps because of uncertainty about what it really now means. So *Lord pour thy Spirit from on high* (AMNS 282) remains in Anglican collections. It is not the best expression of the way in which we understand the ordained ministry, but it must stay until it is replaced by something better. Otherwise we are restricted to more general hymns about Christian service.

On the other hand, there are areas in which poor or dull verses can be replaced by something very much better. The hymn *Lead us heavenly Father, lead us* (doomed from the start when thus introduced) remains a favourite with some — perhaps because they are grateful for what it does say, and unaware that other hymns say the same thing in a better way. One couplet, long open to question, runs:

Lone and dreary, faint and weary,
Through the desert thou didst go

and the second adjective has seemed highly inappropriate when applied to Jesus. Some recent hymn books have felt compelled to offer a revision.

Tempted, taunted yet undaunted
through the desert thou didst go (H&P)

self-denying death defying
thou to Calvary didst go (NEH)

which may be an improvement, though it hardly rescues the hymn.
It is moreover associated with a fairly uninspiring tune — which
Erik Routley went so far as to call 'abominable'.

Now this is a hymn about *guidance*. And this is a subject —
unlike ordination — on which many fine hymns have been written.
Guide me, O thou great Redeemer is certainly far more arresting; on
a similar theme there are several fine modern paraphrases of Psalm
139: especially that of Ian Pitt Watson (H&P 543); but above all,
there is a short hymn by Charles Wesley that is almost flawless
in its construction. Let me quote it fully because it is unknown
in so many parts of the Christian Church.

> *Captain of Israel's host, and Guide*
> *Of all who seek the land above,*
> *Beneath thy shadow we abide.*
> *The cloud of thy protecting love;*
> *Our strength, thy grace; our rule, thy word;*
> *Our end, the glory of the Lord.*
>
> *By thine unerring Spirit led,*
> *We shall not in the desert stray;*
> *We shall not full direction need,*
> *Nor miss our providential way;*
> *As far from danger as from fear,*
> *While love, almighty love, is near.*

If the two hymns are compared, some will find 'Israel's host'
daunting, and need to be reminded of its context. Some will miss
the reference to the earthly life of Jesus, and must be led to see
how this is represented in much modern hymnody. If the hymn
is really wanted for Trinity Sunday, it must be said that Watts'
We give immortal praise (AMNS 520, and happily appearing in more
Anglican collections) and Wesley's *Father, in whom we live* (H&P
4) refer to the work of the three Persons in a more vivid way and
with a more orthodox over-all effect. The desert in Wesley's hymn
is that of the Old Testament; but this is a better general model
for pilgrimage than that of the Judaean wilderness in the Gospels.
But whether or not all this is accepted, it is surely surprising that
whereas *Lead us, heavenly Father* appears in most hymn-books, this
one is in relatively few.

No hymn-book can give unlimited space to any one subject. So as well as asking what are the most popular hymns on a particular subject, we ought also to ask what are the best hymns for it, and which ones are most likely to enlarge and fortify the people of God on their pilgrimage.

D. The hymns that we want

This last section leads us to the final question of what hymns will provide the nourishment that we want as we grow to our full stature in Christ. On such a subject, there are many things to be said, but three which seem to be great importance.

(1) The Tradition of the Church

First, we want hymns which represent the Christian tradition in all its fullness. Hymns are an expression of the communion of saints inasmuch as they unite us with those who have loved and served God in the past as well as with those who seek to love and serve Him now. Many of the hymns that we are likely to use come from those treasuries of devotion which the Christian centuries have accumulated, and we shall be enriched by a broader and deeper knowledge of them. One feature of modern collections is that they have looked for contributions not only from contemporary writers and composers, but from those which have come from traditions of the Christian Church that are different from that which a particular book represents. In the two supplements to *Hymns Ancient and Modern Revised,* Isaac Watts and Charles Wesley were among the largest contributors — which indicates that some Anglicans are beginning to realise how much they have missed by the relatively scanty representation of these writers that is found in some earlier books. Again *Hymns and Psalms*, which admittedly claims to be an ecumenical as well as a Methodist hymn book, has looked to the hymnody of both the Church of England and the Church of Scotland as well as to that which comes from well outside the United Kingdom. Hymns are, in fact, a modest handmaid of the ecumenical movement, and long before that phrase was in use, most of us were singing hymns that originated in traditions other than our own. This is a process that needs to continue and to develop. When different Christian bodies share the same building, they could with advantage share one another's hymn-books and even learn one another's tunes.

But, as we have seen, there are those who find the use of classical hymnody incongruous with modern liturgy. If such hymns are to be sung at all, there arises the question of their 'modernisation', to which hymn-books have responded in different ways. It must be admitted that very few hymns have come to use in *precisely* the form in which they were written. Hymn-writers of the past, like those of the present, frequently alter their own verses, and so do the editors of hymn-books. John Wesley begged that no one would mend his own verses or those of his brother, and declared that they had not the competence to do so; yet he himself did not scruple to change other people's verses, and he stands responsible for turning *Our God, our help in ages past* into the impersonal *O God, our help . . . !* Some hymns, however, would be quite unuseable without amendment. A congregation could not sing the greatest of Charles Wesley's poems *Come, O thou traveller unknown* if it still had the line

> *To me, to all, thy bowels move*

and the substitution of 'mercies' has made its use possible. Slight revisions are necessary where a word has changed in meaning, and others seem desirable in the interests of inclusive language — which concern is already introducing a new style of hymn-writing.

But all this needs to be done sensitively and sparingly. And it is a different matter from the whole re-casting of hymns that has been attempted in the cause of contemporary language. Often, this is a cause of irritation rather than a means of comprehensibility. Those who appreciate both the BCP and the ASB often find the new writing of the latter more attractive and more acceptable than the modernizing of 1662. There is a case for different styles of language in the same act of worship, and this is not so much a novelty as it sometimes seems to be. This is a large subject that concerns the whole of liturgy, but is offered here simply as a defence of classical hymnody.

(2) Hymns for today's world

Secondly, we need hymns and tunes that help us to realise that God is present and active in the world of today. Sometimes this is expressed in classical hymnody; but more often this truth is conveyed through those writers who speak of present concerns and present experiences. We have noted the need of such hymns on themes like world peace or conservation; but we have also noted those modern hymns that bring fresh insights to the abiding truths of the Christian Faith. Every generation needs its own hymns — some of which will survive and be passed on, some of which will not. Some hymns of the 1960s now look decidedly passé — but that is no condemnation of them, since they served the purpose for which they were written. Anything written to describe some challenge of the present situation is inevitably soon dated. Past examples are hymns that expressed the great missionary concern of the nineteenth century; *Hills of the north, rejoice* would in its original version, simply be untrue of our present world, though in this case, its re-writing has saved it from oblivion, and left it wedded to the fine tune which was partly the reason for its popularity. The makers of hymn-books obviously have to be concerned with what will 'last', but they must find room for what is appropriate to their contemporaries, in full realisation that their work will have to be revised by the next generation. Lowther Clarke went so far as to say 'It is not the duty of any generation to provide for its successors.[2] For a hymn book is not merely an anthology of past Christian devotion, but a resource for contemporary worship and aspiration.

(3) Hymns that repay work

Thirdly, our repertoire of hymns must include those which we have to work at. There will be texts that need some pondering, phrases that need some unpacking, and tunes which need a lot of learning. This is bad news for an age which expects instant relief from pain, fast foods and gadgets which reduce all labour to a minimum. This does not mean that hymns should be difficult because that makes them better, or difficult because that is good for us. But any text or music that seeks to explore the glory of God and then in some way to express it is not likely to yield all that it has in an instant. That which is immediately and wholly comprehensible can very quickly become stale. This is why a congregation that is seeking to grow in faith cannot be satisfied with an invariable diet of words that need no pondering and music that can be picked up in a flash. To avoid misunderstanding, let me say again that such songs have a place at some stages in our pilgrimage, and minister to one need of our human nature. But there are other stages of pilgrimage and other needs of our human nature. And just as worship must be carried into work so must work be carried into worship.

This does not mean the advocacy of the Protestant work ethic or middle class values. Nor does it mean that qualifications for worshippers should include at least O levels in English and music. It simply means that we are not for ever to be babes in Christ, that spiritual growth is part of Christian discipleship, and that hymns can be part of that nurture which is needful for us all.

We must not under-estimate the effects of hymns upon us. At the turn of the century, it was the fate of many children to sit through long sermons in church or chapel. One of them turned to the hymn-book for diversion; and so began an interest in hymnody a love of hymns and a discernment and understanding of them that resulted in one of the finest books ever to be written about hymnody.[3]

Very few of those who use hymns are likely to write books about them. And it must be admitted that hymn singing can have results that are far from beneficial. Erik Routley, the greatest hymnologist of this century has said that hymns can 'encourage the slothful to remain slothful, the ignorant to stay ignorant. They can replace faith by complacency, and love by sentimentality.'[4] But they can enlarge our vision, deepen our understanding and strengthen our dedication. Hymns are not necessary to salvation; but they are a means by which we can make it our own.

NOTES

1. This is well discussed in Norman Goldhawk *On Hymns and Hymn Books* (Epworth, 1979), chapter 6; and the subject is always and obviously under review in the bulletins of the Hymn Society of Great Britain and Ireland. And no student of hymnody can ignore the prolific and always stimulating writing of Erik Routley on this subject.

2. Lowther Clarke, *A Hundred Years of Hymns Ancient and Modern* (William Clowes, 1960), p. 79.

3. B.L. Manning, *The Hymns of Wesley and Watts* (Epworth, 1942). The book was reprinted in 1988.

4. Erik Routley, *Christian Hymns Observed* (Mowbrays, 1983), p. 107.

APPENDIX

The Book of Jonah: a sequence of hymns and readings (see p. 62)

	AMNS	H&P	MP
1. The word of God to the prophet Jonah 1:1-2			
Ye servants of God, your Master proclaim	149	278	278
The Lord will come, and not be slow	29	245	
God has spoken by his prophets		64	
2. The prophet's disobedience Jonah 1:7-17			
Dear Lord and Father of mankind	115	673	40
In Adam we have all been one	474	420	
O loving Lord, who art for ever seeking		798	
3. The prophet's deliverance Jonah 2			
Through all the changing scenes of life	209	73	246
God moves in a mysterious way	112	65	
Amazing grace		215	10
4. Mission renewed Jonah 3			
Tell out my soul	422	86	215
Father whose everlasting love		520	
We have heard a joyful sound			255
5. A reluctant missionary Jonah 4:1-18			
Breathe on me, breath of God	157	280	25
Forgive our sins	362	134	
Give to me Lord a thankful heart		548	
When Christ was lifted from the earth	525		
6. God's continuing purpose of mercy Jonah 4:9-11			
Go forth and tell		770	61
We have a gospel to proclaim	431	465	
Jesus shall reign	143	239	125